Cheryl,

   To recognize your excellence in
" Culinary pursuits." Enjoy this Calgary project.
            Joan
A Friend and Calgary "Foods" Teacher

dishing

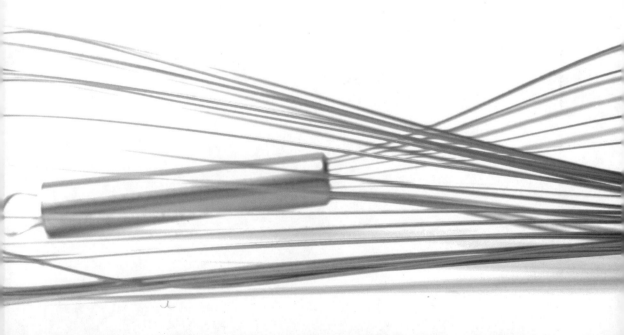

contents

appetizers

Fresh Jalapeño Shortbread

At Christmas time I make thousands of savoury shortbread for clients, always trying to come up with new flavour combinations. Basically, I replaced the heat of cayenne in a spicy cheese shortbread with the fresh jalapeños. That jalapeños just happened to come in two colours, red and green, was probably more than a coincidence! They look great and will please even those wary of hot chilies.

— Karen

Makes 6 to 7 dozen

2 ½ cups	unbleached sifted flour	600 mL
1 tsp.	sea salt	5 mL
½ lb.	good aged cheddar, grated	225 g
½ lb.	unsalted butter, room temperature	225 g
2	each fresh red and green jalapeños, seeded and diced	2

Sift the flour and salt together and set aside. In a large bowl or with an electric mixer, cream together the cheese and butter. Gradually add the dry ingredients and mix until just incorporated (do not overwork the dough). Add the diced jalapeños and mix in.

Divide the dough into 4 pieces. Form into logs about 1 inch (2.5 cm) in diameter. Wrap the logs in waxed paper and chill for at least 1 hour.

Preheat the oven to 350ºF (175ºC). Line 2 baking sheets with parchment paper.

Cut the logs into slices about ¼ inch (.6 cm) thick and place on baking sheets about 2 inches (5 cm) apart. Bake until slightly coloured, about 12 to 14 minutes. Remove from the oven and let cool on wire racks.

Spicy Air-Cured Olives & Alberta Sheep Feta

Serves 4 to 6

1 cup	air-cured black olives	240 mL
½ lb.	sheep feta, cubed	225 g
1 tsp.	grated lemon zest	5 mL
1 Tbsp.	Italian seasoning (or a mixture of oregano, basil and thyme)	15 mL
2	hot dried chilies, crushed	2
¼ tsp.	freshly ground black pepper	1 mL
1 Tbsp.	balsamic vinegar	15 mL
1 tsp.	fennel seed	5 mL
	extra virgin olive oil	

Place the black olives and cubed feta in a jar just large enough to hold them. Add the lemon zest, Italian herbs, crushed chilies, black pepper, balsamic vinegar and fennel seed, then fill the jar with extra virgin olive oil. Place the lid on the jar and shake gently to distribute seasonings. Store in the refrigerator overnight to allow flavours to meld before serving.

Serve with cocktail picks for skewering cheese and olives, along with fresh chewy bread and an extra dish for the olive pits. Alternately, present an olive and cheese chunk on a pick (tapas style) for passing.

This is a great appetizer to have on hand when people visit. It will keep for several weeks in the refrigerator. Serve with a basket of bread for dipping in the seasoned olive oil. In Alberta, a wonderful sheep feta is available from Shepherd Gourmet Dairy— sheep feta is more flavourful than feta made from cow's milk.

— Cinda

Caponata Deluxe

This delicious relish makes a terrific hostess gift. Keep a few jars on hand for a quick hors d'oeuvre, too. Serve with crackers or crostini or to accompany grilled fish and meat.

— Ellen

Makes about 4 cups (1 L)

2–3	eggplants, cut into ¾-inch (2-cm) cubes	2–3
1 Tbsp.	kosher salt	15 mL
2	medium onions, chopped	2
2	cloves garlic, minced	2
1	large fennel bulb, diced	1
½ cup	good-quality olive oil	120 mL
4	sweet red peppers, seeded and diced	4
2 cups	canned plum tomatoes, chopped	480 mL
1 Tbsp.	tomato paste	15 mL
¼ cup	Italian green olives, pitted and chopped	60 mL
¼ cup	small capers	60 mL
1	lemon, zest and juice	1
¼ cup	red wine vinegar	60 mL
1 Tbsp.	sugar	15 mL
2 Tbsp.	each coarsely chopped golden raisins and toasted pine nuts (see page 171)	15 mL
	salt and freshly ground black pepper to taste	

Sprinkle the eggplant cubes with the kosher salt and drain in a colander for about ½ hour. Blot dry with a tea towel or paper towel.

Meanwhile, in a large skillet over medium heat, sauté the onion, garlic and fennel in 1 to 2 Tbsp. (15 to 30 mL) olive oil until soft. Transfer to a large bowl.

In the same skillet, heat 2 to 3 Tbsp. (30 to 45 mL) olive oil and sauté the drained eggplant, adding more oil if needed, for 7 to 10 minutes, until the eggplant is cooked through but still firm. Add the eggplant to the onion mixture in the bowl. Sauté the red peppers in the same manner.

Pour all the cooked vegetables back into the skillet and add the tomatoes, tomato paste, olives, capers and lemon zest and simmer for another 15 minutes. Stir in the lemon juice, vinegar, sugar, raisins and pine nuts and simmer until the liquids have mostly evaporated, about 10 minutes. Season to taste with salt and pepper, remove from the heat and let sit until cooled before serving.

The caponata will keep in the fridge for 2 to 3 weeks. Alternatively, you may can it while it's still hot.

Roasted Red Pepper Hummus

Serves 4 to 6

3 cups	chickpeas (garbanzo beans), drained	720 mL
3	roasted red peppers, seeded, peeled and roughly chopped (see page 54)	3
2 Tbsp.	cumin seed, toasted and ground	30 mL
⅓ cup	tahini paste	80 mL
2 tsp.	sesame oil	10 mL
¼ cup	olive oil	60 mL
2	lemons, juice only	2
3	cloves garlic, minced	3
2 Tbsp.	kosher salt	30 mL

Place all ingredients in the bowl of a food processor and process until smooth, scraping down the sides as necessary. It will last refrigerated for about 6 days.

This makes a great dip for mini-pappadums, pita bread or veggies. I often substitute Gloria Brand Vegetable Spread for the roasted peppers—it tastes great and is ready to use!

—Gail

Bagna Cauda

Serves 4 to 6

¼ cup	butter	60 mL
¼ cup	good-quality olive oil	60 mL
1 lb.	mushrooms, finely chopped or grated (in a food processor)	450 g
6–8	cloves garlic, minced	6–8
4–6	anchovy fillets, drained, rinsed and minced	4–6
1 cup	whipping cream	240 mL
	salt and freshly ground black pepper to taste	

Melt the butter in oil over high heat in a heavy, deep-sided sauté pan. Add the mushrooms, garlic and anchovies. Lower heat to a simmer and add the cream. Simmer 15 to 20 minutes until it is reduced by ¼ and the anchovies are mostly dissolved.

Season to taste with salt and pepper and serve with raw vegetables and crusty bread. Place the bagna cauda over a votive candle to keep it warm—if you think it won't all be eaten within 5 minutes!

Don't let the fat scare you; remember, it's only a dip! Belgian endive makes the perfect accompaniment to this rich warm mixture.

— Ellen

Mediterranean Dip with Herb Pita Chips

This is a great dish to make ahead of time, since the flavours are heightened when they have had a chance to marinate together. You can find roasted red peppers, ready to go, in many stores. However, don't let the roasting procedure intimidate you. It is worth the extra time. Try marinated artichokes and olives, as the oil helps enhance the flavour.

— Judy

Serves 6 to 8

2	roasted red peppers, finely chopped (see page 54)	2
1 cup	artichoke hearts, finely chopped	240 mL
2	green onions, finely chopped	2
⅓ cup	green olives, finely chopped	80 mL
½ cup	black olives, finely chopped	120 mL
¼ cup	capers, finely chopped	60 mL
½ cup	Roma tomatoes, finely chopped	120 mL
1 Tbsp.	parsley, roughly chopped	15 mL
1	lemon, juice only	1
	salt and freshly ground black pepper to taste	
3	cloves garlic, roasted and minced (optional)	3

Place all the ingredients in a bowl and add salt and pepper to taste. Mix thoroughly.

Herb Pita Chips

Serves 6 to 8

¼ cup	olive oil	60 mL
1	clove garlic, minced	1
¼ tsp.	dried thyme	1.2 mL
¼ tsp.	dried oregano	1.2 mL
	salt and freshly ground black pepper to taste	
3–4	fresh pita rounds	3–4

Preheat the oven to 375ºF (190ºC). In a bowl, whisk together the olive oil, garlic, thyme, oregano, salt and pepper. Brush the pita bread with the mixture, and using a sharp knife, cut each pita into 12 pieces. Place on a baking sheet and bake for 10 to 12 minutes, or until lightly browned. Let cool and serve.

Roasting Garlic

Preheat the oven to 375ºF (190ºC). Trim a thin slice from the top of a whole garlic bulb, then drizzle a small amount of olive oil on the cut surface. Place the bulb on a baking sheet and roast, uncovered, for 45 to 60 minutes. Once the garlic bulb is soft to touch, remove it from the oven and gently squeeze out the roasted cloves. The cloves can be left whole, minced, or mashed into a paste.

— Janet Webb

Roasted Eggplant Rolls Stuffed with Chèvre

Serves 4 to 6

2	eggplants	2
	salt	
	olive oil	
8 oz.	chèvre	240 g
2	cloves garlic, minced	2
1	green onion, minced	1
6	basil leaves, julienned	6
	zest of 1 orange, minced	
1–2 Tbsp.	whipping cream	15–30 mL
1–2 tsp.	olive oil	5–10 mL
	salt and freshly ground black pepper to taste	
1 recipe	Roasted Red Pepper Sauce (see page 18)	1 recipe
	whole basil leaves, for garnish	

When I run into people I've catered for in the past, their eyes usually cloud over in ecstasy as they reminisce about this dish. It is luscious and full of flavours that haunt your food-dreams. The crumbly chèvre needs the whipping cream and olive oil to create a creamy filling. Both the sauce and the rolls can be made in advance and reheated prior to assembly.

— Gail

Slice the eggplant lengthwise about ¼ inch (.6 cm) thick. Place the slices in a colander set over a large bowl and sprinkle generously with salt. Allow the eggplant to drain for at least 30 minutes and for as long as 2 hours.

Preheat the oven to 400ºF (200ºC). Generously brush a cookie sheet with olive oil and place the eggplant in the oil, flipping the slices so both sides are oiled. Bake until one side is slightly crispy and brown, about 10 minutes, then flip and brown the other side.

For the chèvre filling, mix together the chèvre, garlic, green onion, julienned basil, orange zest, cream and olive oil, adding just enough whipping cream and olive oil to bind. Season to taste with salt and pepper.

Place 2 generous Tbsp. (30 mL) of the mixture at the end of each eggplant round and roll up. Lay the rolls on an oiled cookie sheet. You can set the rolls aside while you prepare the roasted red pepper sauce.

When you are ready to finish the dish, put the rolls in a 400ºF (200ºC) oven for about 3 minutes to heat briefly. Make sure you don't heat them too much so that the cheese filling begins to melt and run out of the rolls. For each serving, spoon some sauce on a plate, top with two rolls and garnish with a whole basil leaf.

Roasted Red Pepper Sauce

Makes about 2 cups (480 mL)

1 Tbsp.	olive oil	15 mL
1 Tbsp.	butter	15 mL
4	red peppers, roasted, peeled and cut into ½-inch (1-cm) dice (see page 54)	4
1	medium onion, chopped	1
2	cloves garlic, minced	2
1 cup	rich chicken broth	240 mL
4	tomatoes, chopped	4

Heat the olive oil and butter in a pan over medium-high heat. Sauté the roasted pepper, onion and garlic until soft, about 10 minutes. Add the broth and continue cooking until it is reduced to a syrupy consistency. Add the chopped tomatoes to the roasted red pepper mixture and heat through.

Chicken Liver Pâté with Cognac & Figs

Serves 8 to 12

1	onion, minced	1
4	cloves garlic, minced	4
2 Tbsp.	unsalted butter	30 mL
1 lb.	chicken livers, cleaned and patted dry	450 g
½ tsp.	dried basil	2.5 mL
	salt and freshly cracked black pepper to taste	
2–4 Tbsp.	cognac or port	30–60 mL
½ cup	unsalted butter (optional)	120 mL
2–4 Tbsp.	whipping cream (optional)	30–60 mL
¼ cup	minced dried figs	60 mL
2 Tbsp.	minced fresh basil	30 mL

Sauté the onion and garlic over medium-high in the 2 Tbsp. (30 mL) butter until the onion is tender and translucent, about 5 minutes.

Set the onion aside and sauté the chicken livers in small batches until medium-rare, about 3 minutes (until just pink in the centre). Sprinkle each batch with dried basil, salt and pepper to taste. Deglaze the pan with the cognac or port after the last batch is cooked.

Purée the chicken livers in a food processor with the sautéed onion and garlic, blending until perfectly smooth. If desired, add the ½ cup (120 mL) butter in pieces, then stir in the cream, figs and basil. Pack into small ramekins, wrap well and chill. Serve in the ramekins with fresh figs and crusty fig-anise bread.

When making this as a pâté, soften the dried figs if necessary in warm water or orange juice. The finished pâté keeps well, snugly covered, for several days in the fridge. If a warm chicken liver salad is more to your liking, use these components to make a lovely salad on mixed greens or arugula, dressing the result in a sherry vinaigrette.

— dee

Recommended wine:
Alsatian gewurztraminer or
pinot gris, or French Cru Beaujolais

Chicken Liver, Apple & Walnut Mousse

This recipe continues to please and, as an added entertaining bonus, can be made and put into molds and then in the freezer. It is delicious served on toasted pieces of a nutty bread with pieces of toasted walnut and fresh chives as garnish. It also makes a great dip for apple wedges and Belgian endive leaves. If you want to be really decadent, make the mousse with duck livers instead of chicken livers.

— Karen

Serves 20 to 30

1 cup	walnuts	240 mL
3 Tbsp.	walnut oil	45 mL
12	chicken livers, trimmed	12
6	shallots, chopped fine	6
2 Tbsp.	fresh thyme leaves	30 mL
½ cup	Calvados	120 mL
10 Tbsp.	unsalted butter	150 mL
1	large, Red Delicious apple, peeled, cored and thinly sliced	1
½ cup	granulated sugar	120 mL
1 tsp.	sea salt	5 mL
1 tsp.	freshly ground black pepper	5 mL

Toast the walnuts on a baking sheet in a preheated 350°F (175°C) oven for 10 minutes. Remove and let cool.

In a large skillet, heat the walnut oil over medium heat. Add the chicken livers and sauté them until browned, about 4 minutes. Add the shallots and thyme leaves and sauté for 1 minute more. Transfer this mixture to a food processor. Add Calvados to the pan and deglaze for 1 minute. Pour this over the livers in the food processor.

In the skillet, melt the butter over medium-high and add the apple slices. Sauté the apples until they begin to get soft, 8 to 10 minutes, then add the sugar. Continue cooking until the apples are a caramel colour. Add the apples and walnuts, reserving ¼ cup (60 mL) walnuts for garnish, to the ingredients in the food processor. Process until everything is well puréed.

Strain the purée through a fine sieve and season with salt and pepper. Taste and adjust if necessary. The mixture can be packed into a terrine or mold or a plastic wrap–lined loaf pan. Let cool and then refrigerate.

Garnish with the reserved walnuts before serving.

Foie Gras with Cherries & Balsamic Vinegar

Serves 6

⅔ cup	good-quality balsamic vinegar	160 mL
½ cup	dried sour cherries	120 mL
1	baguette, sliced into six ½-inch (1-cm) slices on the diagonal	1
1	lobe foie gras	1

Place the vinegar and cherries in a small pot and simmer 5 to 10 minutes to plump the cherries.

Place a baguette slice on each of 6 small plates.

Heat a cast-iron frying pan to smoking hot. Slice the foie gras into six ¾-inch (2-cm) slices. Place the slices into the hot pan and fry for approximately 3 minutes per side. The outside should be crusty brown but the inside should still be slightly rare.

Place a piece of foie gras on each baguette slice. Spoon 1 to 2 tsp. (5 to 10 mL) of fat from the pan over each slice of foie gras.

Measure ½ cup (120 mL) of hot fat into the cherries and vinegar, and spoon this mixture over each piece of foie gras. Serve immediately.

Spoil yourself with this decadent French classic. It's easier to prepare than you think, and your guests will be very impressed!

— Pam

Foie Gras Bread Pudding with Duck Confit & Sauterne-Soaked Cherries

Decadent is the only appropriate word to describe the ingredients in this first course. The ingredients are toney, but the methods are easy if followed closely. Don't serve a larger portion than the recipe dictates and follow this course with a simple salad, palate-cleansing sorbet or light soup.

— Shelley

Serves 8

1 cup	sun-dried Bing cherries	240 mL
1 cup	Sauterne wine	240 mL
4 cups	dry brioche or "milk" bread, crust removed and cubed	1 L
1 cup	chicken stock	240 mL
½ cup	milk	120 mL
2 tsp.	Dijon mustard	10 mL
2 tsp.	kosher salt	10 mL
4	egg yolks	4
1	egg	1
1	large shallot, finely diced	1
1 Tbsp.	fresh thyme, finely chopped	15 mL
½ lb.	foie gras, membrane removed, veins pulled out	225 g
4	large duck legs, thighs attached, thigh bone removed	4
1 ½ cups	kosher salt	360 mL
1	onion, quartered	1
1	whole bulb garlic, cut in half	1
1	large sprig fresh thyme	1
2	bay leaves	2
¼ cup	whole black peppercorns	60 mL
4 cups	duck fat, melted	1 L

Place the cherries into a tall glass container and cover with the Sauterne. Seal with a leakproof lid and refrigerate. Turn the glass container upside down once a day until all the wine has been absorbed by the cherries (1 to 2 days).

In a large bowl, moisten the bread with the stock.

Scald the milk in a pot with the Dijon mustard and salt. In a bowl, whisk together the egg yolks and eggs.

Slowly whisk the scalded milk into the eggs. Pour the egg-milk mixture over the moistened bread. Add the shallot and thyme. Combine carefully, to avoid breaking up the bread too much.

Crumble the foie gras into pieces equal to the size of the bread bits and fold it into the bread mixture. Cover and refrigerate for 8 to 12 hours. You can begin to prepare the duck confit while the bread pudding mixture chills.

Trim the duck legs of any excess fat around the thigh, and remove the thigh bone if the butcher has not done so. Put the duck legs in a shallow dish and cover with the salt. Refrigerate for 3 to 8 hours to allow the meat to tenderize.

Remove the bread pudding mixture from the fridge and lay out a piece of heatproof plastic wrap (I prefer Resinite) about 12 inches (30 cm) long on a clean countertop. Remove ½ of the bread pudding mixture with a slotted spoon and spread it along the edge of plastic closest to you, at least 3 inches (7.5 cm) from the bottom and 4 inches (10 cm) from each side. Roll the edge closest to you up and around the mixture. Continue rolling, shaping it into a log. Pinch one end and tie a knot in the plastic to close the end. Do the same on the other end, first pushing towards the closed end to compact the ingredients. Rewrap again in several layers of plastic and finally with one layer of aluminum foil. Repeat for the other ½ of the bread pudding mixture.

Preheat the oven to 275°F (135°C). Place the wrapped logs in a baking dish more than large enough to hold them. Fill the baking dish with warm water and bake for 3 to 4 hours. Be sure to turn the logs over several times to ensure even cooking. When done, the bread pudding should be slightly firm to the touch. Remove from the water bath and cool completely before serving.

While the bread pudding is baking, remove the duck from the salt and rinse well under cold running water. Pat the legs dry with clean kitchen towels and place into a roasting pan with the onion, garlic, thyme, bay leaves and peppercorns. Cover with the duck fat and bake for 3 to 4 hours, or until the meat is tender to the point of falling off the bone. Cool and store in the duck fat.

When ready to serve, remove the duck from the fat and shred the meat by pulling it off the bone. Place the shredded confit on a baking sheet and warm in a 400°F (200°C) oven for 8 to 10 minutes.

Cut ½-inch (1.2-cm) slices of the cooled bread pudding and dust with a little flour. Sauté the slices quickly in a very hot pan with butter just until golden brown. Serve 2 to 3 slices per plate, with shredded duck confit and cherries tossed around the plate.

Gravlax on Buckwheat Blini with Flying Fish Roe & Crème Fraîche

This is a luxurious dish that must be started several days in advance. Use salmon, arctic char or steelhead for the gravlax, and indulge yourself. If you can, have your fishmonger cut two fillets from one fish, preferably from the tail, and preferably from opposite sides of the backbone so that they lie together in a perfect fit.

— dee

Serves 12 very generously

2 ¼ lbs.	steelhead or salmon fillet, in 2 pieces of equal size and shape	1 kg
¼ cup	kosher salt	60 mL
¼ cup	white sugar	60 mL
1–2 Tbsp.	Chimayo chili powder or other high-quality chili powder	15–30 mL
2 Tbsp.	minced fresh thyme	30 mL
2 tsp.	freshly cracked black pepper	10 mL
	zest of 1 lemon	
½ cup	pepper-flavoured vodka	120 mL
½ cup	crème fraîche (see page 212 or 216) or sour cream	120 mL
1 Tbsp.	minced fresh dill	15 mL
1 recipe	Buckwheat Blini	1 recipe
1	4-oz. (120-mL) jar flying fish roe (tobiko) or caviar	1
	fresh chives and chive blossoms, for garnish	

To start the gravlax, pull the pinbones out of the fish using a pair of tweezers or needle-nose pliers. Mix together the salt and sugar, then sprinkle it evenly over the fillets. Wrap the pieces, flesh side to flesh side, snugly in plastic wrap and chill, with a drip pan to catch exuded liquids, for 24 to 48 hours. Place full, heavy cans of any food on top of the fish to apply weight.

Unwrap the fish and brush off any undissolved crystals of salt and sugar. Sprinkle the surface with chili powder, thyme, pepper and lemon zest. Drizzle the vodka over the herbs and spices. Wrap and chill for another 12 to 24 hours, then slice thinly on an angle. Combine the crème fraîche or sour cream with the dill.

To serve, spoon a little herbed crème fraîche or sour cream on each blini, top with a gently folded slice of gravlax, then garnish with a small dollop of crème fraîche and a bit of roe. Add a sprig of chives and pull apart a chive blossom, sprinkling the petals over top.

Buckwheat Blini

Tender little pillows, with a slightly pungent buckwheat aroma, these blini are a classic companion for gravlax. If you want, make them bigger and serve them for brunch, topped with slivered smoked salmon or gravlax, sour cream, herbs or fruit syrup.

Makes 24 to 36 blinis

1 Tbsp.	yeast	15 mL
1 Tbsp.	white sugar	15 mL
½ cup	warm milk	120 mL
¾ cup	buckwheat flour	180 mL
½ cup	all-purpose flour	120 mL
2	eggs	2
2 Tbsp.	melted butter	30 mL
	salt to taste	
	additional warm milk as needed to thin the batter	

Combine the yeast, sugar and milk in a mixing bowl. Let stand until frothy, about 5 minutes, then add the flours, eggs, melted butter and salt. Stir in as much milk as needed to make a runny batter about the consistency of pancake batter.

Let rise until it has approximately doubled in volume, then deflate and spoon onto a hot, oiled griddle in small rounds. Turn when bubbly, and cook the other side. Remove to a rack and let cool.

Noodle-Wrapped Prawn & Mango Skewers

Serves 6

18	large prawns, peeled and deveined	18
½ lb.	dried Chinese egg thread noodles	225 g
1	mango, medium ripe	1
18	long wooden skewers	18
2 cups	safflower oil or other suitable oil for frying	480 mL
4 Tbsp.	light brown sugar	60 mL
4 Tbsp.	rice wine vinegar	60 mL
4 Tbsp.	water	60 mL
2 Tbsp.	Thai fish sauce	30 mL
2	red chilies, seeded and diced	2
1 Tbsp.	grated ginger	15 mL

Bring a pot of salted water to a boil and blanch the prawns for 10 seconds, then remove and drain. Be sure the prawns and noodles are well drained and dry.

Soak the dried noodles in a bowl of hot water for 10 minutes, or until soft. Drain well and set aside.

Peel and slice the mango into 1-inch (2.5-cm) cubes. Set aside.

Holding the prawn with the thickest part toward you, push the skewer up through the centre of the prawn and out the top of the thinnest part, leaving 1 inch (2.5 cm) exposed on the end. Repeat the process with all the prawns.

Heat the oil in a straight-sided shallow pan to 375ºF (190ºC). Wrap some of the noodles tightly around each prawn. Deep-fry 2 or 3 noodle-wrapped prawns at a time for 1 to 2 minutes until the noodles are crisp. Thread a cube of mango onto the exposed tip of each skewer.

Repeat the process until all the prawns are fried and threaded with mango, then place them on a baking sheet until ready to serve.

In a small saucepan over medium heat, warm the sugar, vinegar, water, fish sauce, chilies and ginger. Cook until reduced by half. Keep warm.

Preheat the oven to 400ºF (200ºC). Place the tray of prawns into the oven and reheat for 2 to 3 minutes. Place on a serving platter or individual plates and drizzle the warm chili sauce over the prawns.

Prawn, Scallop & Crab Mousse Wrapped in Nori

Serves 8

1 lb.	large sea scallops	450 g
3–4	egg yolks	3–4
1 tsp.	minced fresh tarragon	5 mL
	zest of ½ lemon, finely grated or minced	
¼ cup	whipping cream	60 mL
	salt and cayenne to taste	
2 oz.	raw shrimp, chopped	60 g
2 oz.	crab meat	60 g
8	nori sheets	8
1	tomato, finely diced	1
2 Tbsp.	fennel, finely diced	30 mL
1 Tbsp.	chives, minced	15 mL
1 Tbsp.	basil, minced	15 mL
1 Tbsp.	orange-infused olive oil	15 mL
1 Tbsp.	rice vinegar	15 mL
1 Tbsp.	orange zest, blanched	15 mL
	salt and hot chili flakes to taste	

Clean the scallops by removing the "foot" from each. Set aside 8 perfect scallops and finely purée the rest in a food processor. Add the egg yolks and blend well. Stir in the tarragon, lemon zest, cream, salt, cayenne, shrimp and crab.

Preheat the oven to 325°F (160°C). Butter eight 4-oz. (120-mL) ramekins. Drop a scallop in the bottom of each, then add the seafood mousse to cover.

Place the ramekins in a baking dish filled with enough boiling water to come almost to the top of the ramekins. Cover and steam in the oven until just set, about 20 to 25 minutes. Remove from the oven, uncover and let them stand on a rack for 5 to 10 minutes before unmolding from the ramekin. Wrap each mousse in a strip of nori.

Toss together the tomato, fennel, chives, basil, olive oil, vinegar and zest to make a salpicon. Adjust the balance with salt and hot chili flakes to taste. Spoon the salpicon evenly over the nori-wrapped mousses, drizzling the juices onto the plates. Serve warm.

This evolved from a scallop mousseline I made with Jamie Kennedy, one of Canada's leading chefs, as he presented a beautiful, subtle menu at The Cookbook Company Cooks in Calgary. I have turned it into a fusion dish, wedding the flavours of Nice with a bit of Asian, perfect for a special event's first course. To simplify a bit, omit the nori, and serve the salpicon of tomato and fennel directly over the mousse in the ramekins.

— dee

Shrimps Sautéed with Cilantro Chipotle Butter

The Cilantro Chipotle Butter wonderfully enhances the subtle flavour of the shrimp in this simple dish.

— Gail

Serves 6

18	large shrimps (3 per guest)	18
1 recipe	Cilantro Chipotle Butter	1 recipe

To prepare the shrimp, melt 2 Tbsp. (30 mL) Cilantro Chipotle Butter over medium-high heat in a frying pan. Add a single layer of shrimps to the hot butter. Cook on one side until the shrimps turn pink, about 2 minutes, then flip and finish cooking, about 1 minute.

Add more butter to the frying pan, if required, and cook another round of shrimps. Serve immediately.

Cilantro Chipotle Butter

Make lots of this compound butter—it is so versatile. Use it as a base for a pasta sauce, sauté other fish or seafood in the butter, or brush it on baguette slices to make flavourful crostini.

Makes about 1 cup (240 mL)

1	bunch cilantro	1
4	green onions, roughly chopped	4
2	cloves garlic	2
½ cup	butter, unsalted	120 mL
4 Tbsp.	chipotles in adobo sauce	60 mL
2 Tbsp.	ground cumin	30 mL
	salt and freshly ground black pepper to taste	
⅓ cup	fresh mint, minced (optional)	80 mL

In a food processor, purée the cilantro and green onions until finely minced, then add the remaining ingredients one at a time.

Form into a log or pack into a tub and store in the refrigerator until ready for use. The butter will keep for 1 month refrigerated.

Recommended wine:
marsanne or viognier from
southern France

Lobster Salsa Tartlets

Makes about 70 tartlets

1 ¾ cup	unbleached all-purpose flour	425 mL
pinch	sea salt	pinch
pinch	granulated sugar	pinch
1	egg	1
½ cup	unsalted butter, softened	120 mL
⅓ cup	cold water	80 mL
1 lb.	cooked lobster meat, chopped	450 g
2 Tbsp.	unsalted butter	30 mL
1 recipe	Tomato Salsa with Chervil	1 recipe

To make the dough, mix the flour, salt, sugar, egg and butter in a large bowl or with an electric mixer at low speed. When the ingredients are almost mixed, add the water and continue mixing until blended. (Do not over-work the dough.) Shape the dough into 2 rounds and wrap in plastic wrap. Chill in the refrigerator for 1 hour.

Roll out the dough on a lightly floured surface until about ⅛ inch (.32 cm) thick. Cut out a 1 ½-inch (3.8-cm) round piece of dough and place in 1-inch (2.5-cm) tartlet molds. Refrigerate for 30 minutes.

Preheat the oven to 325ºF (150ºC). Remove tartlet shells from the refrigerator and bake for 12 minutes. Remove from the tartlet molds and let cool on a wire rack.

Sauté the lobster meat in butter over medium heat, just to warm it up slightly. Place one small spoonful of the lobster meat in each tartlet, top with a little salsa and serve.

I use this tart dough for at least a million different fillings. They can be frozen in the tartlet form before they've been cooked, but they do not freeze well after cooking. The tart dough recipe is from Daniel Boulud and seems to work all the time. Experiment with the fillings on your own and amaze your guests at cocktail parties with these elegant bite-sized appetizers. Don't worry if there is leftover salsa' mixture. It's great added to eggs or cooked pasta.

— Karen

Tomato Salsa with Chervil

Makes about 1 cup (240 mL)

4	medium-sized good tomatoes, preferably heirloom in different colours, cut in ¼-inch (.6-cm) dice	4
1	shallot, finely diced	1
1	lime, juice only	1
1	bunch fresh chervil or basil leaves	1
	sea salt and freshly ground black pepper to taste	

In a glass or ceramic bowl, combine all the salsa ingredients.

salads

Fresh Italian Greens

I don't really know why I call these Italian greens except that people do think I should have been born Italian. Other than that, the salad contains fennel and radicchio, Italian components, and a very simple, tart dressing—very Italian. All the textures of the different greens and scents of the herbs combine beautifully for a salad that is fresh, and very refreshing. This is definitely one of those recipes where if you are missing an ingredient, make it anyway!

— Karen

Serves 6 to 8

1	head butter lettuce, separated into leaves	1
1	head romaine lettuce, inner leaves only	1
1	head radicchio, torn into leaves	1
2	Belgian endives, leaves separated	2
1	bunch fresh mint, leaves only	1
1	bunch fresh parsley, leaves only	1
1	bunch fresh basil, leaves only	1

Mix all the greens together, tearing lettuces into smaller pieces if desired.

Vinaigrette

Makes about 1/2 cup (120 mL)

2 tsp.	red wine vinegar	10 mL
2 tsp.	fresh lemon juice	10 mL
5 Tbsp.	extra virgin olive oil	75 mL
1 tsp.	sea salt	5 mL
1 tsp.	freshly ground black pepper	5 mL

Whisk the dressing ingredients together and adjust seasonings if necessary. Inhale the aroma and serve!

grilled sea bass on a bed of pears, fennel & tomato (page 75)

truffle-scented focaccia with taleggio (page 177)

fresh jalapeño shortbread (page 12),
caponata deluxe (page 14) and
spicy air-cured olives & alberta sheep feta (page 13)

truffles (page 214)

Toasted Pecan & Stilton Salad with Citrus Champagne Vinaigrette

Serves 4

1	butter lettuce	1
4 cups	mesclun greens, loosely packed	1 L
1	green onion, finely chopped	1
1	orange, peeled and separated into segments	1
½ cup	toasted pecans (see page 171)	120 mL
½ cup	Citrus Champagne Vinaigrette	120 mL
½ cup	Stilton cheese, crumbled	120 mL

The rich and creamy texture of the Stilton with the toasted pecans brings this salad to life. It's excellent served with sliced, grilled chicken breast or grilled Portobello mushrooms—try it for a light lunch.

— Judy

Tear the butter lettuce into bite-sized pieces and combine with the mesclun greens in a salad bowl. Add the green onion, orange segments, pecans and the vinaigrette and toss lightly. Add the Stilton and toss lightly again before serving.

Citrus Champagne Vinaigrette

This makes more than you need, but it's delicious on any green salad.

Makes 1 ½ cups (360 mL)

½	lemon, juice only	½
1	orange, juice only	1
¼ cup	champagne vinegar	60 mL
1 tsp.	shallots, finely chopped	5 mL
1 tsp.	Dijon mustard	5 mL
½ cup	olive oil	120 mL
	salt and freshly ground black pepper to taste	

Combine the lemon juice, orange juice, vinegar, shallots and mustard in a bowl. Slowly whisk in the oil. Add salt and pepper to taste.

Mixed Greens with Almonds & Candied Citrus-Ginger Threads

Serves 4 to 6

2 cups	whole almonds	480 mL
1	egg white	1
¼ cup	white sugar	60 mL
½ tsp.	cayenne	2.5 mL
½ tsp.	nutmeg	2.5 mL
	salt to taste	
1 recipe	Tangerine Dressing (page 48)	1 recipe
4 Tbsp.	Candied Ginger-Citrus Threads	60 mL
4 cups	mesclun or other tender greens	1 L

Preheat the oven to 300°F (150°C). Put the almonds in a small bowl. In a separate bowl, whisk the egg white thoroughly. Add it to the nuts, mix well, and drain the nuts through a fine sieve, discarding the liquid. Toss the nuts with the sugar, spices and salt and lay out on a tray lined with parchment paper, well spread out in a single layer. Bake for 15 to 20 minutes, stirring occasionally, until golden. Cool, then break apart if needed. Store in the freezer if you aren't serving them immediately, and thaw at room temperature.

Prepare the Tangerine Dressing, halving the amounts listed for the first 5 ingredients (none of this mixture will need to be reserved).

Toss as many almonds as you and your guests would like—about ½ cup (120 mL) per person—with the Tangerine Dressing, candied threads and mesclun. Divide evenly among small plates and serve promptly.

Candied Ginger-Citrus Threads

Use these tender bites of flavour as garnish on desserts—especially
chocolate and fruit—on ice cream, with pork dishes, and as
garnish for smoked salmon dishes. A little goes a long way, so
be sparing . . . what you don't use today will keep indefinitely in
its own syrup!

Makes about ½ cup (120 mL) each

½ cup	ginger root, peeled and thinly sliced	120 mL
½ cup	citrus zest, coloured part only, thinly sliced	120 mL
	cold water	
1 cup	white sugar	240 mL

Put the ginger and zest into separate small pots, cover
with cold water and bring to a boil. Drain. Replace the
water and repeat the process twice more.

After the third time, add ½ cup (120 mL) of white sugar
to each pot and bring to a boil. Simmer the threads in
the syrup until the fruit is tender, adding more water
as needed.

Pour each potful of threads and syrup into a different
small glass jar while hot, let stand uncovered until
cool, then cover and store.

For sugar-rolled threads, dry the strands on a rack,
then roll in berry sugar or puréed white sugar.

Hot & Creamy Caesar Salad

Serves 4

8	cloves garlic, roasted in skin (see page 16)	8
1	lemon, juice only	1
1 tsp.	Dijon mustard	5 mL
1 tsp.	sea salt	5 mL
1 Tbsp.	cracked black pepper	15 mL
1 tsp.	granulated sugar	5 mL
½ cup	olive oil	120 mL
1–2 Tbsp.	whipping cream	15–30 mL
4	heads romaine lettuce, outer leaves removed	4

When the garlic cloves are cool enough to handle, slip them out of their skins. If they are very soft, they can be mashed; otherwise chop them coarsely.

Make the dressing by combining and whisking all the ingredients except the olive oil, cream and romaine. Slowly add the olive oil in a stream until it has emulsified, then add cream to taste. Adjust seasonings if necessary.

Cut the romaine heads in half. On a hot barbecue or grill, grill the lettuce halves on both sides, being careful not to burn the outer leaves. Place the grilled halves on plates and, while still hot, drizzle the dressing over them.

Beet & Fennel Salad with Two Citruses & Vanilla

Serves 4 to 6

10	medium beets	10
⅓ cup	olive oil	80 mL
2	1-inch (2.5-cm) pieces vanilla bean, split and seeds scraped out	2
1	lemon, juice and zest	1
1	orange, juice and zest	1
1 Tbsp.	sherry vinegar	15 mL
	salt and freshly ground black pepper to taste	
1	medium fennel bulb, thinly sliced	1

Preheat the oven to 400ºF (200ºC). Trim the beets, leaving the tops intact but removing the gnarly top edges, leaving most of the skin on. Bake until a knife can pierce to the centre, about 45 minutes. Remove from the oven and let sit until cool enough to handle, then cut off the tops and tails and cut into large chunks. (You can leave the skins on for a sweeter flavour, or peel them if you prefer.)

In a large serving bowl, mix together the olive oil and vanilla bean. Slowly whisk in the juice and zest of the lemon and orange, then the sherry vinegar. Season with salt and pepper.

Add the beets to the vinaigrette, then add the fennel and mix gently. Adjust the seasonings if necessary. Serve at room temperature or slightly chilled.

Whenever you roast vegetables with their jackets on, their flavour seems to become magnified. I love serving beets that have been oven-roasted in this way. My guests always exclaim, "What have you done to these beets?" When I tell them the "secret," they always look at me askance, thinking I am not telling them the whole truth—but I am!

— Gail

Orzo Wild Rice Artichoke Salad

Great on a buffet table. A little goes a long way, but leftovers will be welcome.

— Ellen

Serves 6 to 8

1	14-oz. (398-mL) can baby artichokes, drained	1
1 recipe	Red Onion Vinaigrette	1 recipe
¼ cup	dried wild rice	60 mL
2 cups	dried orzo	480 mL
¼ cup	mint and parsley, chopped	60 mL
	romaine lettuce, inside leaves	
	lemon juice	
	freshly ground black pepper	
	fresh mint, for garnish	

Marinate the artichokes in the vinaigrette for 2 to 3 hours on the counter or overnight in the refrigerator.

In a small pot, combine the wild rice with 1 cup (240 mL) water and ¼ tsp. (1 mL) salt. Bring to a boil, cover and simmer over low heat until the grains have burst their shells and are fluffy, 50 to 60 minutes. Drain off excess water and set aside.

Bring a large pot of salted water to a boil. Stir in the orzo and cook at a boil until it is al dente, 8 to 10 minutes. Drain and set aside.

Combine the artichokes, wild rice, orzo, mint and parsley and let stand at room temperature for 1 to 2 hours to marry the flavours. Reseason if necessary.

Toss a few small romaine leaves in some lemon juice and pepper and fan out on a plate. Serve a scoop of salad on the leaves and garnish with a sprig of mint.

Red Onion Vinaigrette

Makes about 1 ½ cups (360 mL)

¼ cup	finely diced red onion	60 mL
⅔ cup	good-quality olive oil	160 mL
½ cup	red wine vinegar	120 mL
1 Tbsp.	brown sugar	15 mL
2	cloves garlic, minced	2
½ tsp.	ground cumin	2.5 mL
½ tsp.	dried Mexican oregano	2.5 mL
	salt and freshly ground black pepper to taste	

Whisk all the ingredients together in a glass or ceramic dish with a lid.

Couscous Salad with Tomatoes & Fresh Herbs

Serves 4 to 6

1 cup	couscous (see page 142)	240 mL
1 cup	boiling water, stock or apple juice	240 mL
5 Tbsp.	olive oil	75 mL
½ cup	chopped mint or basil, or a combination	120 mL
5 Tbsp.	apple cider vinegar	75 mL
2	cloves garlic, minced	2
6	Roma tomatoes, chopped	6
¼ cup	crumbled strong cheese, such as Asiago or blue cheese (optional)	60 mL

Place the couscous in a heatproof bowl. Add the boiling liquid to the bowl, cover and set aside for about 10 minutes.

Mix together the olive oil, herbs, vinegar and garlic. Add to the cooked couscous, fluffing the grains, then stir in the tomatoes and cheese, if desired. Serve warm or chilled.

This is a great side dish when your mint patch has gone crazy. It also makes a great picnic dish.

— Gail

Recommended wine:
fruity dolcetto (slightly chilled)
or pinot grigio

Grilled Vegetable Pasta Salad

This salad tastes like summer to me: smoky eggplant and peppers, tomatoes and fresh basil. It is delicious on its own, or served with grilled Italian sausages or lamb chops. Japanese eggplant makes a nice change from globe eggplant. I've also added grilled corn cut from the cob, grilled asparagus, grilled fennel . . .

— Pam

Serves 4

¼ cup	balsamic vinegar	60 mL
¾ cup	extra virgin olive oil	180 mL
1	globe eggplant, sliced lengthwise into ½-inch (1.2-cm) slices	1
2	red peppers, cut in half lengthwise, cored and seeded	2
2	yellow peppers, cut in half lengthwise, cored and seeded	2
1	large red onion, quartered vertically without peeling	1
6	Roma tomatoes	6
1	whole bulb garlic	1
1 lb.	dried pasta (penne, raddiatore, etc.)	450 g
1 cup	Asiago cheese, grated	240 mL
½ cup	chopped fresh basil	120 mL
	salt and freshly ground black pepper to taste	

Preheat the barbecue to medium-high. Set a large pot of salted water on to boil.

Combine the balsamic vinegar and ½ cup (120 mL) olive oil in a bowl.

Place the vegetables on the hot grill and brush with oil and vinegar. Grill until each vegetable is tender and charred to your liking, and until the tomatoes and garlic are soft. Remove each from the grill as they are done.

When the water comes to a boil, add the pasta and cook at a rolling boil for 8 to 10 minutes, until the pasta is al dente. When it is cooked, drain and rinse the pasta and put into a large serving bowl.

Peel the onion and remove the root. Squeeze the garlic into the bowl. Chop the remaining vegetables into bite-sized pieces and add to the bowl. Drizzle with the remaining oil and vinegar, the grated cheese and basil and mix well. Taste and season with salt and pepper. Serve warm or at room temperature.

Warm Bean & Goat Cheese Salad on Wilted Greens

Serves 4 to 6

¾ cup	dried small white beans or pale green flageolet beans	180 mL
1 tsp.	fennel seeds	5 mL
1 tsp.	mustard seeds	5 mL
¼ tsp.	salt	1 mL
1	dried red chili pepper, crushed	1
2 Tbsp.	balsamic vinegar	30 mL
1 Tbsp.	Dijon mustard	15 mL
1 tsp.	honey	5 mL
1 Tbsp.	basil pesto	15 mL
¼ cup	extra virgin olive oil	60 mL
½ lb.	firm aged goat cheese, such as crottin or tome de chèvre, in ¼-inch (.6-cm) cubes	225 g
4	green onions, chopped	4
4–5 cups	mixed sturdy and flavourful greens (mustard greens, watercress leaves, arugula, beet greens, dandelion, chard, etc.)	1–1.25 L
	fresh basil leaves, for garnish	
	freshly ground black pepper to taste	

Use a good surface-ripened or aged goat cheese in this salad, one that will hold its shape and provide a contrast to the beans. Several excellent varieties are available from Natricia Dairy, where artisan goat cheeses are produced with the same care as their famous French counterparts.

— Cinda

Soak the beans for several hours or overnight, then cook in plenty of water until tender, 1 to 2 hours, depending on the age and dryness of the beans.

Meanwhile, to make the dressing, combine the fennel seed, mustard seed, salt, chili pepper, vinegar, mustard, honey and pesto in a food processor and process until the seeds are crushed. Add the olive oil and process to combine. Place the dressing in a large bowl.

When the beans are tender, drain well and toss with the dressing while hot. Add the goat cheese and toss again—the cheese should just start to soften, but not melt. Toss in the green onions.

Tear the greens and arrange on 4 individual plates. Top with some of the warm bean salad. To serve family-style, simply toss the greens with the warm beans. Serve the salad warm and wilted, garnished with fresh basil and a good grinding of black pepper.

White Bean Salad with Mango Chutney & Crystallized Ginger

The combination of chutney and crystallized ginger is wonderful and can be used in other ways. Try this recipe with pasta instead of beans. The bacon adds a layer of flavour, but can be omitted if you prefer.

— Gail

Serves 6 to 8

3 cups	white beans, cooked and cooled (the uncooked measure is 1 cup/ 240 mL of dried beans, see page 154)	720 mL
3	slices bacon, sautéed until crisp, drained and crumbled	3
1	small onion, minced	1
3 Tbsp.	olive oil	45 mL
2 Tbsp.	white wine vinegar	30 mL
	salt and freshly ground black pepper to taste	
½ cup	minced fresh parsley	120 mL
3 Tbsp.	minced crystallized ginger	45 mL
2 Tbsp.	walnuts	30 mL
¼ cup	chopped cilantro	60 mL
3 Tbsp.	mango chutney	45 mL

Place the beans in a salad bowl and add the bacon and onion. Briefly purée the remaining ingredients in a blender. Toss gently with the beans to combine. Chill, covered, for 1 hour. Toss again and serve.

White Bean & Asiago Salad

Typical of this kind of salad, it just keeps getting better as it sits. Make it the night before without the cheese and basil and reseason before serving for the best results.

— Ellen

Serves 6 to 8

4 cups	cooked northern white beans	1 L
2 cups	Roma tomatoes, diced and drained	480 mL
¾ cup	olive oil	180 mL
¼ cup	red wine vinegar	60 mL
1	clove garlic, minced	1
	salt and freshly ground black pepper to taste	
1 cup	fresh basil	240 mL
¾ cup	crumbled Asiago cheese	180 mL

Combine all the ingredients except the basil and Asiago and let sit at least an hour at room temperature.

When ready to serve, cut the basil chiffonade-style by rolling the leaves up together in a tight bundle and slicing into thin strips. Add the cheese and basil just before serving.

Crab & Shrimp Salad with Beet Chips

Serves 4

½ lb.	cooked crabmeat	225 g
½ lb.	cooked shrimp	225 g
½	red pepper, finely chopped	½
½	yellow pepper, finely chopped	½
1	green onion, finely chopped	1
4 oz.	cream cheese, softened	115 g
½ cup	mayonnaise	120 mL
1 Tbsp.	dill, roughly chopped	15 mL
½ tsp.	hot pepper sauce	2.5 mL
1 tsp.	Worcestershire sauce	5 mL
1	lemon, zest and juice	1
½ cup	whipping cream	120 mL
	salt and freshly ground black pepper to taste	
4 cups	lettuce or spring greens	1 L

Flake the crabmeat into a bowl and add the shrimp, peppers and green onion. Set aside.

In a separate bowl, cream together the cheese, mayonnaise, dill, hot pepper sauce, Worcestershire, lemon zest and juice. Add the crab and shrimp to the cream cheese mixture, then the cream, and salt and pepper to taste.

Arrange the lettuce or greens on individual serving plates and mound the crab and shrimp salad in the centre. Surround the salad with beet chips.

Beet Chips

Makes about 1 cup (240 mL)

1	large beetroot	1
	vegetable oil	

Peel the beetroot. Slice as thinly as possible, then blanch in boiling salted water for 60 seconds. Drain and rinse under cold water, and let dry on paper towels.

Put at least 1 ½ inches (4 cm) of oil in a deep pot or fryer and heat to 375°F (190°C). If you don't have a cooking thermometer, carefully take a large slice of beet and put the tip in the oil. If it bubbles as soon as it touches the oil, the pan is ready. Fry the chips in the oil, a few at a time, until crispy. Remove with a slotted spoon and drain onto paper towels. Season with salt and pepper to taste. Serve immediately or let cool and store in an airtight container.

I'm not an authority on deep frying, but the flavour of the beet chips with crab and shrimp makes this recipe special. The combined tastes are truly delicious.

— Judy

Calamari Salad with Fennel

Many people who think they don't like squid have had it overcooked, resulting in a rubber band–like texture. Stand over the pot for this one and time it carefully! This salad is wonderful served with slices of good-quality baguette.

— Pam

Serves 8 as an appetizer, 4 as a light lunch

2 lbs.	cleaned squid tubes, sliced in ¼-inch (.6-cm) rings	1 kg
5	cloves garlic, peeled and thinly sliced	5
pinch	red chili pepper flakes	pinch
½ cup	olive oil, or to taste	120 mL
1	lemon, juice and zest	1
3 cups	fennel, julienned	720 mL
2 Tbsp.	chopped Italian parsley	30 mL
	freshly ground black pepper to taste	

Bring a large pot of salted water to a boil. Divide the squid into 4 equal portions.

In a small saucepan over medium heat, stir the garlic and chili flakes in the olive oil for 4 to 5 minutes. You want to release the flavour without browning the garlic. Pour the mixture into a glass bowl large enough to hold the salad.

Blanch the squid in 4 batches, boiling each batch for 15 seconds. Remove with a sieve, being careful not to overcook. Immediately place the squid in the olive oil mixture and toss. Cook the remaining batches of squid and add them to the bowl.

Add the lemon juice and zest, fennel, parsley and black pepper. Serve warm or chilled.

Arugula Salad with Grilled Chicken, Toasted Peanuts & Thai Dressing

Makes 4 as an entrée or 6 as an appetizer

2	large, boneless, skinless chicken breasts	2
1 recipe	Thai Dressing	1 recipe
4 cups	arugula, stemmed	1 L
	salt and freshly ground black pepper to taste	
1/4 cup	raw, unsalted, skinless peanuts, lightly toasted and roughly chopped (see page 171)	60 mL

Marinate the chicken breasts in 1/2 cup (120 mL) of the Thai Dressing for 30 minutes or up to 2 hours in the refrigerator. (The chicken breasts take on more heat the longer they are in the marinade.)

Heat the grill to medium-high. Grill the chicken breasts, turning once, until cooked through, about 10 to 15 minutes. Allow the chicken to sit for 5 to 10 minutes, then slice on the bias when just warm.

Toss the remaining dressing with the greens and season with salt and pepper to taste. Arrange the greens on a serving plate, top with the chicken slices and garnish with the toasted peanuts.

Arugula (a.k.a. roquette or rocket) is my favourite green! I love the bitter, peppery quality so much so that I plant lots, and my garden yields enough arugula to keep me happy all summer. In winter, this lovely green is difficult to find, and I often replace it with baby spinach or mesclun greens. For a change from chicken, substitute beef or pork tenderloin or shrimp for equally great results.

— Janet

Thai Dressing

Makes 1 cup (240 mL)

2 Tbsp.	hot chili oil	30 mL
2 Tbsp.	sesame oil	30 mL
1	clove garlic, minced	1
1/3 cup	rice vinegar	80 mL
3 Tbsp.	tamari	45 mL
1/4 cup	olive oil	60 mL
1	dried chili, crushed (optional)	1

Combine the chili oil, sesame oil, garlic, rice vinegar and tamari in a small bowl. Let stand for 30 minutes, then slowly whisk in the olive oil. Add the crushed chili, if desired.

Cajun Chicken Liver Salad

I've made more converts to chicken livers with this recipe than I can count. Use more or less Cajun Spice depending on how spicy you like things. The Japanese crumbs give the livers a wonderful texture, but you can use ordinary crumbs if that's all you have.

— Ellen

Serves 6

1 lb.	fresh chicken livers	450 g
1 cup	Japanese-style (Panko) bread crumbs	240 mL
1 Tbsp.	Cajun Spice	15 mL
2	eggs	2
¼ cup	milk	60 mL
1 cup	flour	240 mL
1 Tbsp.	each olive oil and butter	15 mL
	mixed salad greens	
½ recipe	Honey Caper Vinaigrette, or to taste	½ recipe
	salad garnish (carrot, celery, red pepper, fennel, tomato, red cabbage, red onion, etc.)	

Preheat the oven to 350°F (175°C). Trim the livers, removing the whitish membrane and halving the lobes where necessary. Mix the bread crumbs with the Cajun Spice mixture. Whisk the eggs with the milk.

Dredge the livers in flour, then in the egg mixture, and then in the bread crumbs. Use one hand for the flour and egg and the other to cover the livers in crumbs or your fingers will be battered instead of the livers.

Heat the oil and butter over medium-high heat and fry the livers in batches, about 3 to 5 minutes per batch. The livers should be rare inside. Finish cooking in the oven until just pink inside, about 7 to 10 minutes.

Serve 4 or 5 hot livers over the salad greens tossed with the vinaigrette to taste. Garnish with your choice of fresh vegetables. Leftover livers are great cold in a sandwich or served as an appetizer with a creamy dip.

Honey Caper Vinaigrette

This is the dressing I use most often. I usually make more than I need just to have it on hand in the refrigerator.

Makes ¾ cup (180 mL)

2	large cloves garlic	2
1 tsp.	capers	5 mL
½ tsp.	salt	2.5 mL
1 tsp.	Dijon mustard	5 mL
1 tsp.	honey	5 mL
	freshly ground black pepper to taste	
1 tsp.	lemon juice	5 mL
¼ cup	apple cider vinegar	60 mL
	olive oil to taste (about ½ cup/ 120 mL)	

Crush the garlic and capers with the salt. Add the mustard, honey, pepper, lemon juice and vinegar. Whisk in oil gradually until emulsified.

Cajun Spice

My thanks to Paul Prudhomme for introducing me to cooking with various spice mixtures. You'll be surprised at the number of ways you can use this mélange. Share the cost with a friend and make a whack at a time.

Makes about ¼ cup (60 mL)

2 tsp.	salt	10 mL
2 tsp.	cayenne	10 mL
2 tsp.	paprika	10 mL
2	bay leaves	2
1 tsp.	black pepper	5 mL
1 tsp.	rosemary	5 mL
1 tsp.	oregano	5 mL
1 tsp.	chilies	5 mL
½ tsp.	white pepper	2.5 mL
½ tsp.	garlic powder	2.5 mL
½ tsp.	celery salt	2.5 mL
½ tsp.	ground allspice	2.5 mL

Combine all the ingredients in a food processor and grind to a powdery consistency. I usually make a large amount at a time, as it keeps well. Put a damp tea towel over the machine while it's running to keep some of the powder out of the air.

Put in a jar or resealable plastic bag and store as you would any spice, in a cool, dark, dry place.

Recommended wine:
California malvasia or
New Zealand sauvignon blanc

Mango & Duck Salad with Tangerine Dressing

This salad is a singing symphony of synergistic flavours. It makes a perfect light meal, is extremely popular at potlucks, and can be happily partnered by bowls of beans when the weather is chilly.

— dee

Serves 2 to 6

2	boneless duck breasts, skin on	2
1 recipe	Tangerine Dressing	1 recipe
	salt and hot chili flakes to taste	
4 cups	mesclun	1 L
2	mangoes, peeled and diced into ½-inch (1-cm) cubes	2
1 cup	whole almonds, toasted (see page 171)	240 mL

Split the duck breasts along their natural division, then trim them lengthwise, leaving 1 inch (2.5 cm) of fat down the centre of each half. Rub half of the star anise–ginger mixture from the Tangerine Dressing over the duck breasts.

Grill the duck breasts to medium-rare, about 5 minutes on each side, remove from the heat, and let stand 10 to 15 minutes. (See Steak Touch Test, page 95, for a guide to doneness.)

Season the cooked duck with salt and hot chili flakes and trim off the skin if it has blackened. Dice the breasts into ½-inch (1-cm) cubes and toss with the mesclun, mangoes, almonds and Tangerine Dressing. Serve immediately.

Tangerine Dressing

Makes about ¾ cup (180 mL)

1 tsp.	ground star anise	5 mL
2 tsp.	grated ginger root	10 mL
1 tsp.	olive oil	5 mL
4 tsp.	maple syrup	20 mL
2 tsp.	finely grated tangerine zest	10 mL
3–4 Tbsp.	sunflower oil	45–60 mL
⅓ cup	tangerine juice	80 mL
3–4 Tbsp.	lemon juice	45–60 mL
	salt and hot chili flakes to taste	

Combine the star anise, ginger, olive oil, maple syrup and zest in a small bowl. Set aside half of this mixture to use as a rub for the duck.

Put the remaining mixture into a small pan and stir over high heat for 1 minute. Remove from the heat and add the sunflower oil, citrus juices, salt and chili flakes. Mix well to combine.

soups

Vegetarian Minestrone

If your diet is anything like mine, you occasionally have days when the only vegetable that you've ingested is the lettuce on your sandwich! Try mixing up a big batch of this soup to sit on your stovetop so you can grab a bowl on the fly.

— Rhondda

Serves 10

⅓ cup	olive oil	80 mL
3	red onions, chopped	3
4	stalks celery, coarsely chopped	4
4	carrots, coarsely chopped	4
1	small cabbage, shredded	1
7	cloves garlic, coarsely chopped	7
4 cups	tomatoes, stewed or tinned	1 L
8 cups	water	2 L
1	bunch parsley, chopped	1
4 ½ lbs.	Swiss chard, leaves and stalks coarsely chopped	2 kg
	salt and freshly ground black pepper to taste	
3 Tbsp.	fresh thyme, chopped	45 mL

Heat the olive oil in a large saucepan over medium heat and slowly sauté the onions, celery, carrots, cabbage and garlic. Next add the tomatoes, water, half the parsley and the Swiss chard stalks.

Bring to a boil, then simmer for half an hour. Add the remaining parsley, Swiss chard leaves, salt, pepper and thyme. Bring the soup back up to a boil briefly and serve.

Minestrone with Beans: Add 2 cups (480 mL) cooked kidney beans toward the end of the cooking time for a heartier soup.

Roasted Garlic & Pepper Soup with Basil Oil

Serves 6 to 8 as an appetizer, 4 as an entrée

1	whole bulb garlic, roasted (see page 16)	1
3 Tbsp.	olive oil	45 mL
2 ½ lbs.	red bell peppers, roasted (see page 54)	1 kg
1	yellow onion, diced	1
1 Tbsp.	olive oil	15 mL
2 ½ cups	stock (chicken or vegetable)	600 mL
	salt and freshly ground black pepper to taste	
	fresh lemon juice to taste	
½ cup	sour cream	120 mL
2–3	fresh basil sprigs, finely chopped	2–3
2 Tbsp.	Basil Oil (see page 54)	30 mL

Sauté the onion in a large stockpot over medium heat with 1 Tbsp. (15 mL) olive oil until the onion is soft and translucent, about 10 minutes.

Add the roasted garlic and peppers to the onion and sauté over medium heat for 5 to 10 minutes. Add the stock and simmer for 15 to 20 minutes to blend the flavours. Allow the mixture to cool, then transfer in small batches to a blender or food processor. Purée the soup and return it to the stockpot. Add salt, pepper and lemon juice to taste.

Ladle the soup into bowls, add a dollop of sour cream, top with some fresh basil and drizzle each serving with a little Basil Oil.

This can be a heart-warming fireside soup for the middle of winter, or a delightfully refreshing chilled soup for a warm summer's day. I first had a soup like this on a trip through Spain, where peppers are a mainstay. Roasted peppers were served with every meal, and I came to love their earthy, full-flavoured presence. This is my version.

— Janet

Basil Oil

Store the leftover oil in a cool place. Use it in place of unflavoured oil wherever a basil flavour would complement your dish.

Makes about 1 cup (240 mL)

2 cups	fresh basil leaves	480 mL
1 cup	olive oil	240 mL

In a food processor or blender, combine the basil and half the olive oil. Process, scraping down the sides if necessary, until the basil is partially puréed. With the motor running, gradually add the remaining oil through the top.

Transfer to a container, cover and let sit at room temperature for 2 days. Pour the oil through a fine strainer, pressing the purée with the back of a spoon to extract all the flavour. This oil can be refrigerated for 2 to 3 weeks, but must be brought to room temperature before using.

Roasting Peppers

Roasting peppers can be done in three ways: on your barbecue, in your oven, or on your gas element. Lightly rub a little olive oil on the peppers before you roast them.

To roast them in the oven, preheat it to 450°F (220°C), then set the peppers on the top rack. To barbecue peppers, preheat the grill to high, then set the peppers on the grill. If you are doing them on a gas element, place them directly on the flame.

Once the outside of the peppers is blackened, place them in a paper bag or a bowl covered with plastic wrap and set aside to cool. Once cooled, discard the black part of the skin, the stem and seeds. Lightly rinse the pepper under cold water to completely clean the skin.

— Judy Wood

Recommended wine:
Alsatian pinot blanc

Pear, Avocado & Sweet Potato Bisque

Serves 8

1 Tbsp.	olive oil	15 mL
1	small white onion, diced	1
1	medium carrot, peeled and chopped	1
2	stalks celery, diced	2
2	cloves garlic, minced	2
8 cups	chicken stock	2 L
1	orange-fleshed sweet potato, peeled and diced, about 3 cups (720 mL)	1
3 Tbsp.	butter	45 mL
1 Tbsp.	fresh lime juice	15 mL
¾ cup	half-and-half cream	180 mL
1	avocado, peeled and finely diced	1
1	pear or apple pear, peeled and finely diced	1
	zest of 1 lime	

This rich, creamy soup is an elegant first course for a fall feast. The crisp, fresh pear and smooth avocado add an interesting contrast of textures and flavours.

— Cinda

Sauté the onion, carrot, celery and garlic in olive oil in a large soup pot over medium heat for 10 minutes until very tender, but do not brown.

Add the stock and sweet potato and bring to a boil. Cover, reduce the heat and simmer slowly until the sweet potatoes are fork-tender, about 30 minutes.

Cool the soup slightly and blend the solids with some of the broth in a food processor until very smooth. Return the purée to the pot.

Whisk in the butter and lime juice. Add the cream and bring just to a boil. Simmer 3 minutes. Just before serving, stir in the finely diced avocado and pear. Serve each bowl topped with a few strands of lime zest.

Cold Lemon Buttermilk Soup

This is a recipe from my days at the Calgary Golf and Country Club under Chef Brian Plunkett. If a chilled soup doesn't appeal to you, try pouring a thinned and thoroughly iced version in tall glasses with straws and mint sprigs for a refreshing drink.

— Ellen

Serves 6

8	egg yolks	8
2 Tbsp.	sugar	30 mL
2 cups	buttermilk	480 mL
5	lemons, juice only	5
¼ cup	white wine	60 mL
1 cup	whipping cream	240 mL
	lemon zest and fresh mint, for garnish	

Beat the egg yolks with the sugar until light coloured and creamy. Add the buttermilk and mix well. Add the lemon juice and wine.

Beat the cream until thick, but not stiff. Fold it into the soup mixture. Chill and serve garnished with lemon zest and mint.

Celeriac Soup with Black Truffles & Cilantro Oil

Makes sixteen ¹/₂-cup (120-mL) servings

3 Tbsp.	truffle oil	45 mL
2 Tbsp.	unsalted butter	30 mL
2 lbs.	celery root, peeled and cut into medium dice	1 kg
1	medium onion, cut into small dice	1
2	cloves garlic, minced	2
½ lb.	table potatoes, peeled and diced	225 g
2	black truffles, finely julienned	2
4 cups	chicken or vegetable stock	1 L
	kosher salt and white pepper to taste	
¼ cup	fresh lemon juice	60 mL
2 cups	whipping cream	480 mL
	Cilantro Oil (see page 58), for garnish	

In a heavy-bottomed stockpot, heat the oil and butter over medium heat. Gently sauté the celery root and onion until they begin to soften, then stir in the garlic. Add the potatoes and ¹/₃ of the truffles, then add the stock. Season to taste with salt and pepper, and allow the soup to simmer uncovered for 20 to 30 minutes, until all the vegetables are soft. Test by piercing with a paring knife.

Remove the soup from the stove and purée in batches, using a blender, food processor or food mill. Press the purée through a fine-mesh sieve into a clean pot, using the bottom of a ladle to push it through. Reheat the purée to a simmer, then stir in the remaining truffles and the lemon juice. Stir in the cream and adjust seasonings if necessary.

Serve in small bowls drizzled with Cilantro Oil.

It's hard to imagine that two of the most unappealing-looking ingredients can come together so beautifully as these do. Truffles are more and more readily available in specialty food shops; late fall to midwinter is when you are likely to find them fresh. I often buy them "IQF" (individually quick-frozen)—although not as intense in flavour and aroma, they are still quite good. This is a special soup, best served in smaller than normal quantities as a prelude to a fine meal.

— Shelley

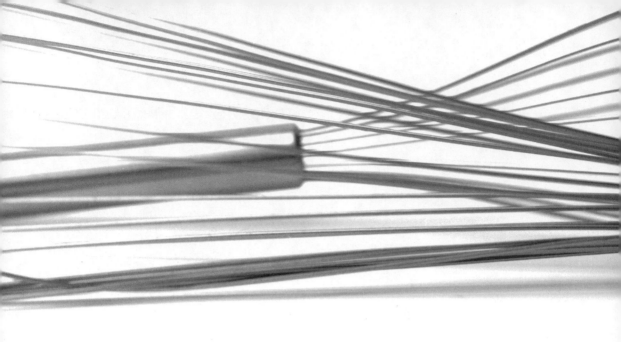

Cilantro or Chive Oil

Flavoured oils not only add flavour, but can be used like "paints" to add colour and movement to the presentation. Herb oils are the easiest to make. Not all herbs work, however—basil, rosemary and tarragon tend to go brown. Chives, cilantro, parsley, watercress and arugula, alone or in combination, all have great colour and flavour.

Makes about 2 ¹/₂ cups (600 mL)

2 cups	fresh cilantro or chives, well packed	480 mL
2 cups	neutral-flavoured oil, such as grapeseed, canola or safflower	480 mL

Bring a pot of salted water to a boil. Blanch the herbs for 5 seconds, then immediately shock in ice-cold water and drain. Chop the herbs and squeeze out excess water.

Purée the herbs with the oil in a food processor in 30-second intervals, stopping to rest the machine's motor, for a total of 3 minutes. Pour into a bowl, cover and refrigerate for 1 day.

Strain the oil through a fine-mesh sieve lined with cheesecloth. You can discard the solids or reserve them for another use, such as flavouring soup stock. Put the oil in a plastic squeeze bottle with a fine tip for the best garnishing results.

Sorrel Potato Soup Two Ways

Serves 4

2 Tbsp.	olive oil	30 mL
1 Tbsp.	unsalted butter	15 mL
8	medium potatoes, skin on, cut into ½-inch (1-cm) dice	8
2	large leeks, including the white part and tender green portion, chopped	2
8 cups	chicken or vegetable stock	2 L
2 cups	sorrel leaves, packed	480 mL
	salt and freshly ground black pepper to taste	
½ cup	Crème Fraîche (see page 212) or sour cream	120 mL
2 Tbsp.	fresh chives (blossoms if possible), for garnish	30 mL

In a large stockpot, heat the olive oil and butter over medium heat until the butter melts. Add the potatoes and leeks, and sauté until the leeks are soft and fragrant, about 5 to 10 minutes.

Add the stock and cook until the potatoes are tender, about 15 to 20 minutes. Add half the sorrel and cook for another 5 minutes. Season to taste with salt and pepper.

To serve, ladle soup into preheated bowls, and stir 2 to 3 Tbsp. (30 to 45 mL) of the remaining sorrel into each bowl. Top with a dollop of Crème Fraîche or sour cream and garnish with chives.

Sorrel Soup with Capicolla: Sauté 4 slices of capicolla over medium-high heat until slightly browned. After the first addition of sorrel, purée the soup in batches until smooth, and return to the stockpot. Chop 3 slices of the capicolla, add it to the stockpot, and cook for another 10 to 15 minutes to incorporate the flavours. Serve as above, sprinkling the remaining chopped slice of capicolla over top of the Crème Fraîche.

Any gardener who grows sorrel knows that the more you use it the more it grows. I have very happy sorrel in my garden, but luckily one of my all-time favourite soups is this one, which is quick, full of earthy flavours and healthy to boot! The first version is vegetarian, keeping the base as a broth. The second, more elegant in style, is puréed, with bits of sautéed capicolla ham as a garnish.

— Janet

Recommended wine:
red—Cru Beaujolais or pinot noir;
white—marsanne/roussane

Wild Mushroom & Wild Rice Soup

Good soup is uncomplicated and simple, not much like life most of the time. This one is an autumn special, perfect when the chanterelles arrive. If you only have dried mushrooms, rehydrate them, use them . . . and don't apologize!

— dee

Serves 4

1 Tbsp.	olive oil	15 mL
½	yellow onion, minced	½
2	carrots, diced	2
4	cloves garlic, minced	4
½	red pepper, diced	½
10–15	mushrooms, sliced	10–15
handful	dried wild mushrooms	handful
¼ cup	wild rice	60 mL
4 cups	chicken, veal or vegetable stock	1 L
2 Tbsp.	sherry	30 mL
½ cup	whipping cream (optional)	120 mL
	salt and freshly ground black pepper to taste	
	minced fresh chives, for garnish	

Heat the oil in a heavy-bottomed pot over medium-high, then add the onion, carrots, garlic and red pepper. Cook until the vegetables are tender, about 5 minutes, adding small amounts of water as needed to prevent burning. Stir in the fresh and dried mushrooms and cook for several minutes more.

Add the wild rice and stock and bring to a boil. Cover and simmer about 40 minutes, or until the rice is tender. Stir in the sherry, cream if desired, and salt and pepper to taste. Serve, garnished with minced fresh chives.

Butternut Squash Soup with Roasted Garlic & Fresh Thyme

Serves 6 to 8

2	medium bulbs garlic	2
1 Tbsp.	olive oil	15 mL
1	medium onion, peeled and coarsely chopped	1
2	medium potatoes, peeled and coarsely chopped	2
1 ½ lbs.	butternut squash, peeled and coarsely chopped	675 g
6 cups	chicken stock	1.5 L
2	bay leaves	2
1 Tbsp.	fresh thyme	15 mL
½ cup	whipping cream	120 mL
	salt and freshly ground black pepper to taste	

Butternut squash not only has a great taste but is easy to work with. You can easily substitute other squash—for example, acorn squash—but you might have to bake them first to be able to remove the flesh. Don't shy away from using the whole amount of garlic. The flavour is fantastic!

— Judy

Place the garlic bulbs on a baking sheet and bake at 350°F (175°C) for 45 minutes. Remove from the oven, cut the tops off and gently squeeze the cloves out.

Heat the oil in a pan. Add the onions and cook over medium heat until they are soft, about 3 to 5 minutes, making sure the pan doesn't become too hot and cause the onions to brown.

Add the garlic, potatoes, squash, stock and bay leaves and cook at a slow boil for 25 minutes. Remove the bay leaves.

Purée the soup in batches and return it to the pot. Bring to a simmer over medium-high heat, then add the thyme, cream, salt and pepper.

Roasted Parsnip, Shallot & Vanilla Bean Soup with Vanilla Crème Fraîche

*In my opinion, most root veget-
ables are grossly underrated. The
natural sweetness, creamness
and rich colour of parsnips give
this recipe its luxurious taste and
texture. Most root vegetables
contain some fibrous bits, so
don't skip the straining—it refines
the end result for a smooth finish.*

— Shelley

Serves 6

2 Tbsp.	unsalted butter	30 mL
1 Tbsp.	olive oil	15 mL
3 lbs.	parsnips, peeled and diced	1.3 kg
1	whole vanilla bean, split and seeds scraped out	1
6–8	shallots, peeled and quartered	6–8
2	cloves garlic, peeled and quartered	2
1 tsp.	ground cumin	5 mL
	kosher salt and freshly ground white pepper to taste	
4 cups	chicken or vegetable stock	1 L
1 cup	whipping cream	240 mL
1/2 cup	Vanilla Crème Fraîche (page 212)	120 mL

In a heavy-bottomed pot over medium-high heat, melt the butter with the oil. Add the parsnips, vanilla bean and seeds, shallots and garlic. Cook, stirring constantly, until the vegetables caramelize and soften, about 20 to 30 minutes. Add the cumin, salt and pepper and stock. Simmer, uncovered, until the vegetables are completely soft, about 20 minutes. Remove the vanilla bean.

Working in batches, purée the soup in a blender or food processor until smooth. Using a fine-mesh sieve, strain the soup into a clean pot, using the back of a ladle to press the purée through. Discard the solids left in the sieve.

Stir in the whipping cream and heat through, then adjust the seasonings if necessary. Serve with drizzles of Vanilla Crème Fraîche on top.

Vanilla Beans

Avoid buying vanilla beans that are dry, hard and brittle, as they are old and have little flavour. Beans are best stored in the fridge in tightly sealed, thick plastic bags inside a sealed glass jar. Fresh, whole beans can last for six months. Alternatively, store whole beans in a jar of sugar or in vodka or rum. The beans in sugar will remain drier and more pure in flavour than those stored in liquor.

A hard vanilla bean can be revitalized by immersing it in hot water or in vodka or rum until pliable.

To prepare the beans for cooking, remove the seeds by splitting the bean lengthwise, using a paring knife. Separate the halves and flatten. Run the blade along the cut side of the bean to scrape the seeds out.

— Gail Norton

Recommended wine:
New World chenin blanc or
fruity New World dry riesling

Salmon Sorrel Chowder

Serves 6 to 8

2 lbs.	salmon heads and tails	900 g
6 cups	water	1.5 L
	salt to taste	
	several sprigs thyme	
1	leek, coarsely chopped	1
1	carrot, sliced	1
1	celery stalk, chopped	1
1	lemon, halved	1
½ cup	dry white wine	120 mL
1	bay leaf	1
8–10	black peppercorns	8–10
3 lbs.	salmon fillet	1.3 kg
1 Tbsp.	good-quality olive oil	15 mL
½ cup	finely chopped shallots	120 mL
½ lb.	fresh sorrel, washed and chopped	225 g
¼ cup	butter	60 mL
½ cup	flour	120 mL
½ cup	dry white wine	120 mL
	reserved fish stock	
1 cup	whipping cream	240 mL
	salt and white pepper to taste	
	fresh chervil, for garnish	

Rich and elegant with its green and pink colours, this soup makes a lovely first course. Although you could use spinach instead, it's the tart lemony flavour of the sorrel that sets this chowder apart.

— Ellen

Place the salmon heads and tails in a large saucepan. Add the water, salt, thyme, leek, carrot, celery, lemon, wine, bay leaf and peppercorns. Bring to a boil, reduce the heat and simmer, covered, for 20 minutes. Add the salmon fillet and gently poach for 10 minutes. Remove the fish from the court bouillon and set aside. Strain and reserve the stock, discarding the solids.

Heat the olive oil in a large soup kettle on medium-high and sauté the shallots until soft. Add the sorrel and sauté until the sorrel has cooked down, about 7 to 10 minutes. Add the butter. When melted, stir in the flour. Cook, stirring, for 5 minutes or so, until the roux is well incorporated and foamy. Pour the wine in while whisking to prevent lumps. Add enough of the fish stock to thin to a heavy cream consistency and continue to simmer to concentrate the flavours and reduce slightly, about 15 minutes. Add the cream. Season to taste with salt and pepper.

Break the salmon fillet into pieces and add to the soup. Cook for another 10 minutes to heat thoroughly. Garnish with fresh chervil.

Blackened Seafood Chowder

The term "blackened" comes from New Orleans and means that the meat or fish has been coated in Cajun Rub, then cooked in a red-hot cast-iron pan. You can use the seafood of your choice for this chowder. It makes a great meal on a cold day, served with a rustic sourdough bun.

— Judy

Serves 6 to 8

4 Tbsp.	butter	60 mL
2	cloves garlic	2
1	medium onion, peeled and coarsely diced	1
2	celery stalks, coarsely diced	2
1	medium red pepper, seeded and coarsely diced	1
3 Tbsp.	flour	45 mL
4 cups	fish stock, heated	1 L
3	medium potatoes, peeled and coarsely chopped	3
2	bay leaves	2
¼ cup	Cajun Rub	60 mL
¼ lb.	prawns, peeled	115 g
¼ lb.	scallops	115 g
¼ lb.	mussels, shelled	115 g
¼ cup	clams, shelled	115 g
1 cup	whipping cream	240 mL
	salt and freshly ground black pepper to taste	

Heat the butter in a pan over medium heat. Add the garlic and onion and cook until soft, about 3 to 5 minutes, being careful not to brown the vegetables. Add the celery and diced pepper and cook, stirring often, for about 5 minutes.

Reduce the heat to low, add the flour and stir to make a roux. Cook for 5 minutes, then slowly stir in the fish stock. Add the potatoes and bay leaves and cook at a slow boil for 20 minutes.

Heat a cast-iron pan over medium-high heat. Coat the seafood with Cajun Rub and toss in the preheated pan. Cook for only 2 to 3 minutes. Add the seafood to the soup, where it will finish cooking.

Bring to a simmer over medium-high heat, then add the cream, salt and pepper. Serve hot.

Cajun Rub

This recipe makes more than you need for the chowder, but it
keeps for about 3 months. Try this rub when cooking all kinds of
meats and fish.

Makes 1 cup (240 mL)

⅓ cup	paprika	80 mL
2 Tbsp.	onion powder	30 mL
2 Tbsp.	garlic powder	30 mL
2 Tbsp.	cayenne	30 mL
1 Tbsp.	pepper	15 mL
3 Tbsp.	thyme	45 mL
3 Tbsp.	oregano	45 mL

Mix the spices together thoroughly and store in
an airtight container.

Ward's Crab Bisque

Serves 8

8	prawns, peeled and quartered (reserve the shells)	8
2 Tbsp.	cilantro leaves	30 mL
1 tsp.	curry powder	5 mL
1 Tbsp.	safflower oil	15 mL
4 slices	cold-smoked salmon, slivered	4 slices
6 cups	crab shells (about 8 crabs)	1.5 L
¼ cup	unsalted butter	60 mL
3	kaffir lime leaves	3
2 Tbsp.	mild Hungarian paprika	30 mL
	water or fish stock to cover	
2 Tbsp.	unsalted butter	30 mL
1	onion, finely minced	1
3	cloves garlic, minced	3
3	kaffir lime leaves	3
1	lime, juice and zest	1
2	carrots, minced	2
1 tsp.	curry powder	5 mL
½ tsp.	ground cumin	2.5 mL
¼ tsp.	fenugreek	1.2 mL
¼ tsp.	ground coriander	1.2 mL
1 cup	white wine	240 mL
¼ cup	tomato paste	60 mL
	shell stock, strained	
2–4 Tbsp.	cornstarch	30–60 mL
1	lemon, juice only	1
	salt and hot pepper sauce to taste	
½ cup	whipping cream	120 mL
¼ cup	grappa	60 mL

In a small bowl, combine the peeled prawns, cilantro, 1 tsp. (5 mL) curry powder, oil and smoked salmon. Mix well, then chill until needed to garnish the soup.

Add the prawn shells to the crab shells.

In a heavy-bottomed stock pot over medium heat, combine the reserved prawn shells, the crab shells, ¼ cup (60 mL) butter, 3 lime leaves and paprika. Stir often and cook until aromatic and the shells are ruddy-coloured.

Add cold water or fish stock to just cover the shells. Simmer for 30 to 40 minutes, then taste the shell stock. If it is too thin in flavour, simmer it to reduce and concentrate the flavour, then strain and discard the solids. Taste again and reserve the stock.

Clean the pot, then melt the 2 Tbsp. (30 mL) butter over high heat. Add the onion, garlic, 3 lime leaves, lime juice and zest, carrots, 1 tsp. (5 mL) curry powder, cumin, fenugreek and coriander. Reduce the heat to medium and cook, stirring, for 5 to 7 minutes, or until the onion and carrots are tender. Do not allow the vegetables to brown more than a very little bit.

Mix in the wine and tomato paste, then simmer the mixture for several minutes. Add the shell stock and simmer for 10 to 15 minutes.

Dissolve the cornstarch in a little cold water. Bring the soup to a boil, add the dissolved cornstarch and stir. The soup should thicken almost immediately. Add more cornstarch dissolved in water, if it isn't thick enough for your liking.

Stir in the lemon juice, salt, hot pepper sauce, whipping cream and grappa. Bring to a boil, taste, rebalance the flavours if necessary, and keep hot.

Heat a non-stick sauté pan over medium-high. Remove the prawn and smoked salmon mixture from the fridge. Sauté the mixture very quickly until the prawns are just cooked, about 3 minutes, then season with salt and pepper.

Ladle the soup into heated bowls, divide the seafood garnish evenly among the servings, and serve hot with crusty bread.

Curry Powder

Curry powder is used mainly in dishes from southern India, and can include coriander, cumin, mustard seed, fenugreek, hot chilies, peppercorns and turmeric. Cinnamon and cloves added create a Moghul-style curry. You can prepare your own curry powder or buy a commercial blend.

— dee Hobsbawn-Smith

Recommended wine:
Tuscan sangiovese, cabernet
blend or simple Chianti reserva

Pasta e Fagioli (alla moda Katarina)

Who needs another beans and pasta soup recipe? Well, maybe nobody, but I always love learning from someone who cooks from the soul. This is what I learned from one of my favourite cooks, Katarina Caraciola from the Italian Centre in Calgary. She generously let me stand behind her one day when she was preparing this universal dish. This meal has as many recipes as there are cooks and I truly hope my soup does her justice because I may have made some changes inadvertently. She says the biggest argument in her family is over which pasta to use.

— Karen

Serves 6

1 lb.	dried cannellini beans	450 g
5 Tbsp.	olive oil	75 mL
¼ lb.	spicy pancetta, coarsely diced	112 g
¼ lb.	prosciutto, coarsely diced	112 g
2	cloves garlic, minced	2
½ tsp.	dried red chilies	2.5 mL
¼ cup	white wine	60 mL
2	tomatoes, chopped	2
1	sprig fresh rosemary, chopped	1
	sea salt and freshly ground black pepper to taste	
½ lb.	dried pasta (tubetti or shells)	225 g
	fresh Parmesan, shaved	
	extra virgin olive oil	

Soak the beans overnight in enough cold water to cover. Drain off the soaking liquid and place the beans in a large stockpot. Cover them with water, bring to a boil, then turn down the heat and simmer until tender. Depending on the beans, this will take 1 to 2 hours. When tender, drain off any remaining liquid, but reserve it. Let the beans cool. When cool, return the beans to the cooking liquid. This may be done a few days ahead and the beans will benefit from sitting in the refrigerator in the cooking liquid.

In a large sauté pan heat the olive oil over medium-high heat. Add the pancetta and prosciutto and sauté until most of the fat is rendered from the meat. Add the garlic and sauté for 1 minute. Add the chilies and sauté for 1 minute more. Add the wine and reduce for 2 minutes, then add the tomatoes and rosemary and continue to cook for about 5 minutes more.

Add the cooked beans and about ¼ of the cooking liquid, or enough to cover, and salt and pepper to taste. Simmer for about 20 minutes.

While the soup is simmering, heat a large pot of salted water to a boil. Add the dried pasta and cook at a rolling boil for about 10 minutes. It should still be quite al dente.

Add the pasta to the soup and toss gently. Adjust seasonings if necessary.

Serve in wide soup bowls with shavings of Parmesan and drizzled with olive oil.

Quick Bean Soup with Pancetta & Roasted Garlic

Serves 4 to 6

1	whole bulb garlic	1
½ cup	olive oil	120 mL
6 slices	pancetta, chopped	6 slices
2 Tbsp.	parsley, chopped	30 mL
2	24-oz. (720-mL) cans white kidney beans, drained	2
2 cups	chicken or vegetable stock	480 mL
	salt and freshly ground black pepper to taste	

Preheat the oven to 450ºF (230ºC). Remove a thin slice from the top of the garlic bulb, drizzle the cut surface of the bulb with a little olive oil, place in a small pan and cover with foil. Roast in the oven for 30 to 45 minutes until the garlic is soft and fragrant. Remove from the oven, uncover and let cool.

Heat the remaining olive oil over medium-high in a large stockpot. Add the pancetta and sauté until crisp, about 15 minutes. Add the parsley, and cook for 1 to 2 minutes. Add the drained beans and squeeze the garlic out of its papery skin into the stockpot. Add the stock and simmer for 10 minutes. Add salt and pepper to taste.

Purée 1 cup (240 mL) of the beans and stock in a blender or food processor. Return the purée to the soup. Simmer for another 5 minutes and serve hot.

This is rib-sticking soup, soup that cures colds, makes lousy days better and soothes a broken heart. Lots of beans, mellow roasted garlic and little nips of salty pancetta are all thrown together in less than 60 minutes. It can be made as a vegetarian soup by using vegetable stock and omitting the pancetta. Serve alongside toasted Italian ciabatta bread and a small salad, and the world will be a better place.

— Janet

entrées

Mussels with Fennel

*This is a dish I crave in winter
when mussels are in season. Use
a "drinkable" wine, and serve
with a glass of the same wine
and some crusty bread.*

— Pam

Serves 2

3 Tbsp.	extra virgin olive oil	45 mL
3	cloves garlic, peeled and thinly sliced	3
1 lb.	fresh fennel, trimmed and julienned	450 g
4	plum tomatoes, cored and chopped	4
¼ tsp.	aniseed, crushed	1.2 mL
2 cups	sauvignon blanc	480 mL
	chili flakes to taste	
	freshly ground black pepper to taste	
2 lbs.	fresh mussels, debearded	1 kg

Heat the oil on medium-high in a pan large enough to hold the mussels after they open. Sauté the garlic without colouring it. Add the fennel and cook until softened, about 10 to 15 minutes. Add the tomatoes, aniseed and wine. Season with chili flakes and black pepper. Use caution with salt, as the mussels will add salt with their liquor.

Simmer 5 minutes to cook the tomatoes and blend the flavours. The recipe may be made in advance to this point. Reheat to simmering to proceed.

Add the mussels, cover and cook until they open, about 5 minutes. Do not overcook. Discard any mussels that do not open.

Ladle the mussels in their shells into serving bowls, along with fennel and broth.

Glazed Sea Bass with Red Curry Sauce & Braised Baby Bok Choy

Serves 8

3 Tbsp.	peanut or vegetable oil	45 mL
1 tsp.	sesame oil	5 mL
8	4-oz. (125-g) Chilean sea bass fillets, skin on	8
¼ cup	cornstarch	60 mL
¾ cup	chicken stock	180 mL
⅓ cup	honey	80 mL
⅓ cup	soy sauce	80 mL
3 Tbsp.	lime juice	45 mL
¼ tsp.	red chili paste	1 mL
1	clove garlic, minced	1
	cilantro sprigs, for garnish	
1 recipe	Braised Baby Bok Choy (see page 74)	1 recipe
1 recipe	Red Curry Sauce (see page 74)	1 recipe

We serve this delicate glazed fish atop a pile of fragrant jasmine rice. The spicy coconut curry sauce is delicious drizzled over the fish, rice and vegetables.

— Cinda

Heat the oils in a large non-stick pan over high heat. Dust the fillets with cornstarch and sauté, skin side up, over medium-high heat for 4 minutes or until crisp and golden. Transfer the fish, skin side down, to a large rimmed baking sheet that has been rubbed with oil.

Make a glaze by combining the remaining ingredients, except the cilantro, in a saucepan. Simmer until reduced to ⅓ cup (80 mL).

Spoon 1 Tbsp. (15 mL) glaze over each piece of fish and bake in a 400°F (200°C) oven until just cooked, about 8 minutes. Serve the fish over Braised Baby Bok Choy, drizzled with Red Curry Sauce and garnished with the cilantro sprigs.

Braised Baby Bok Choy with Shiitake Mushrooms

Serves 8

8	baby bok choy, sliced in half lengthwise	8
2 Tbsp.	unsalted butter or ghee	30 mL
2	cloves garlic, minced	2
1 lb.	shiitake or Portobello mushrooms, sliced	450 g
2 cups	chicken stock	480 mL
1	star anise	1
	salt and freshly ground black pepper to taste	

Rinse the bok choy under cold water to remove any grit. Drain and dry well.

Melt the butter in a heavy non-stick skillet over medium-high heat. Add the garlic and sauté for 1 minute. Add the bok choy, cut side down, and the mushrooms, and sauté for 2 minutes, until beginning to brown.

Add the stock and star anise and boil until the bok choy and mushrooms are tender and the stock is reduced and thickened, about 8 to 10 minutes. Season with salt and pepper to taste.

Remove the star anise before serving.

Red Curry Sauce

You can make your own Thai curry pastes, but it's easier to buy premade pastes at Asian groceries or supermarkets. Thai curry pastes may be red, green or yellow and are sold in foil pouches and small tubs. Fish sauce is also available in Asian stores.

Makes about 2 cups (480 mL)

2 Tbsp.	Thai red curry paste	30 mL
1 cup	coconut milk	240 mL
1 tsp.	fish sauce	5 mL
1 tsp.	brown sugar	5 mL
1 cup	chicken broth	240 mL
2 Tbsp.	lime juice	30 mL
2 Tbsp.	chopped cilantro	30 mL

Simmer all the ingredients except the cilantro until slightly thick, about 15 minutes. Stir in the cilantro just before serving.

Recommended wine:
French Chablis

Grilled Sea Bass on a Bed of Pears, Fennel & Tomatoes

Serves 4

1 Tbsp.	olive oil	15 mL
4	8-oz. (170-g) sea bass fillets	4
1	fennel bulb, trimmed	1
2	pears, cored and sliced	2
1/2 lb.	teardrop tomatoes, washed	225 g
1	lemon, juice only	1
1 Tbsp.	golden corn syrup	15 mL
1/4 cup	olive oil	60 mL
	salt and freshly ground black pepper to taste	

The crispness of the fennel helps soften the rich flavour of the sea bass. The teardrop or pear tomato is slightly smaller than a cherry tomato. They look good, but can be replaced with another kind of tomato if you prefer.

— Judy

Rub the olive oil onto the sea bass and set aside while the grill or barbecue heats to medium-high.

Remove the outside layer and any brown layers from the outside of the fennel bulb. Cut the bulb in half, slice it thinly and put it into a bowl. Slice the pears thick enough so they won't fall apart when they're tossed together. Add the tomatoes and pears to the fennel.

In a separate bowl, combine the lemon juice and corn syrup and whisk in the oil. Season with salt and pepper. Add the dressing to the fennel mixture and toss well. Set aside.

Preheat the oven to 350°F (175°C). When grilling the sea bass, make sure the grill is very clean and very hot before putting the fish on it. Use the grill just to quick-mark and flavour the fish, 1 1/2 minutes on each side. Transfer the fillets to a baking dish and bake for 5 to 10 minutes in the oven until cooked through.

Arrange the fennel mixture on a serving plate and lay the fish on top.

Salmon with Roasted Artichoke, Tomato & Olive Sauce

I'm always looking for new ways to serve salmon. It has fast become the most requested dinner item. I love serving salmon with strong flavours because the oil content in the fish stands up so well to bold tastes. I saw a recipe for salmon with an "artichoke sauce à la greque" which required the tedious (to me) preparation of fresh artichokes and sauce. Having recently tried some fabulous roasted artichokes that came in a jar, I decided to skip the fresh, go with roasted and do the Greek part with the tomatoes and olives. Bingo! If you can't find roasted artichokes, you can use marinated artichokes—drain them and roast in a 425°F (220°C) oven for about 10 minutes.

— Karen

Serves 4

12	roasted artichokes, quartered	12
2	cloves garlic, chopped	2
2 Tbsp.	fresh lemon juice	30 mL
1/3 cup	extra virgin olive oil	80 mL
4	salmon fillets	4
	sea salt and freshly ground black pepper to taste	
4	tomatoes, seeded and cut into 1/4-inch (.6-cm) dice	4
1/2 cup	kalamata olives, pitted and slivered	120 mL
4 Tbsp.	fresh parsley (or basil), finely chopped	60 mL

In a food processor, combine 6 artichokes, the garlic and lemon juice and process until you have a smooth paste. Add the olive oil in a drizzle and process until the sauce is emulsified. It should be thick but liquidy enough to sauce a plate. Strain through a sieve into a small saucepan.

Preheat the oven to 450°F (230°C). Place the salmon on a baking sheet lined with aluminum foil. Salt and pepper the salmon and bake for 8 to 10 minutes, depending on thickness, until the salmon flakes easily or reaches your desired degree of doneness. If you prefer, the salmon can also be barbecued.

While the salmon is cooking, gently heat the artichoke sauce and add the tomatoes and olives. Place the cooked fillets in the centre of four warm dinner plates and spoon sauce around them. Sprinkle the remaining artichoke quarters onto the plates and scatter parsley over all.

Lavender Fennel–Crusted Salmon with Roasted Baby Potatoes

Serves 4

2 Tbsp.	lavender	30 mL
2 Tbsp.	whole fennel seeds	30 mL
2 Tbsp.	freshly ground coarse pepper	30 mL
1 tsp.	kosher salt	5 mL
2 cups	baby "creamer" potatoes	480 mL
1 Tbsp.	olive oil	15 mL
	kosher salt to taste	
1 ½ lbs.	centre-cut salmon fillet, pinbones removed	680 g
1 Tbsp.	olive oil	15 mL
½ lb.	arugula leaves, washed and trimmed	225 g
1 recipe	Elderflower Marigold Vinaigrette (see page 78)	1 recipe

*The crust for the salmon was inspired by Chef John Ash in his wonderful book **From the Earth to the Table**. I've added lavender, which creates a delicious flavour complement when combined with the elderflower vinaigrette. Toss in some roasted potatoes and fresh arugula and you have one of the most popular items I've ever put on a menu.*

— Shelley

Combine the lavender, fennel seeds, pepper and 1 tsp. (5 mL) salt in a small bowl. Set aside.

Preheat the oven to 400ºF (200ºC). Toss the potatoes in 1 Tbsp. (15 mL) olive oil and season with salt. Place on a baking sheet and roast for 15 to 20 minutes, stirring occasionally, until they are crisp on the outside and tender in the middle.

Cut the salmon into equal size portions, keeping the skin on. Place a baking sheet into the preheated oven for 10 minutes. Lightly brush the flesh side of each salmon portion with olive oil. Make a crust of the prepared spices on the flesh side of the salmon. Place the flesh side down onto the hot baking sheet. Once placed on the sheet, do not try to move the salmon, as it will be stuck at first. Bake the salmon for about 5 minutes, then flip and bake for another 3 minutes. Remove from the tray to serve.

Put the clean arugula in a large bowl. Add the hot potatoes and about ¼ cup (60 mL) of Elderflower Marigold Vinaigrette, and toss to coat well. Divide among serving plates and top each plate with a portion of salmon.

Elderflower Marigold Vinaigrette

This will make more dressing than you need for this dish, but it will keep for up to 2 weeks in the fridge. Use it to enhance any green salad.

Makes about 1 ¾ cups (420 mL)

1	shallot, peeled and finely minced	1
1 Tbsp.	Dijon mustard	15 mL
1	egg yolk	1
1 Tbsp.	fresh lemon juice	15 mL
1 Tbsp.	white wine	15 mL
½ cup	elderflower cordial	120 mL
¼ cup	marigold petals, dry	60 mL
	kosher salt	
1 cup	mild olive oil	240 mL

In a food processor or blender, place the shallot, Dijon mustard, egg yolk, lemon juice, wine and elderflower cordial. Process the mixture until combined. Add the marigold petals and salt to taste.

With the machine running slowly, add the oil in a steady stream. Check the seasoning. If not using right away, place the vinaigrette in a container in the fridge.

Cedar-Planked Salmon with Dill Beurre Blanc

Serves 4

4	cedar planks, untreated	4
4	6-oz. (170-g) salmon fillets	4
1 recipe	Dill Beurre Blanc	1 recipe
	salt and freshly ground black pepper to taste	

Soak the planks in cold water for at least 1 hour, or overnight.

Preheat the barbecue to medium-high or 350°F (175°C). Lay the salmon fillets on top of the wood and brush a small amount of Dill Beurre Blanc Sauce over top. Season with salt and pepper, then set the plank onto the barbecue. Cook with the lid down for 10 to 15 minutes, until it feels firm to the touch or flakes easily with a fork. Be careful not to overcook. Check on the plank regularly. You should have a squirt bottle of water at hand to put out a fire, in case one starts.

Slide the fillets off the wood and serve with the sauce lightly drizzled over the top.

Dill Beurre Blanc

Makes 1 cup (240 mL)

2 Tbsp.	butter	30 mL
3	shallots, finely chopped	3
1 ½ cups	dry white wine	360 mL
1 Tbsp.	lime juice	15 mL
3 Tbsp.	whipping cream	45 mL
2 Tbsp.	fresh dill, finely chopped	30 mL
⅔ cup	cold butter, cut into small cubes	160 mL
	salt and freshly ground black pepper to taste	

Heat the butter in a pan over low heat. Add the shallots and cook for 3 minutes. Add the white wine and lime juice and reduce until the liquid has almost disappeared. Add the cream and dill and bring to a boil, then remove from the heat.

Whisk in the butter until it is melted and smooth. Season with salt and pepper.

If you can afford to throw the cedar plank on the barbecue, you get great flavour from the smoke of the burning wood. If you want a more subtle flavour, the oven is a good alternative. For an outdoor barbecue, we set a presoaked piece of wood in the centre of each table. When the salmon was ready, the planks were placed on top of the other piece of wood.

— Judy

Recommended wine:
fruity South African or
New Zealand sauvignon blanc

Brined Atlantic Salmon with Wine Gastrique

Succulent and tender, brined salmon is a favourite in my home. Cook it on the grill or in a hot oven. Don't hold your breath looking for leftovers. For an awesome appetizer, serve small pieces of this fish on shards of Crackers with Coarse Salt and Seeds (page 188), with or without Six-Fruit Chutney (page 117). This marinade adapts tremendously well to pork loin; leave the loin in the marinade overnight, then roast or grill the meat and garnish it with fruit chutney or an aïoli.

— dee

Serves 6

1 ½ cups	dry white wine	360 mL
¼ cup	white sugar	60 mL
2 Tbsp.	kosher salt	30 mL
2 tsp.	coriander seed	10 mL
2 tsp.	fennel seed	10 mL
2 tsp.	mustard seed	10 mL
1 Tbsp.	black peppercorns	15 mL
3	bay or kaffir lime leaves	3
1 Tbsp.	finely sliced fresh ginger	15 mL
1	star anise	1
	zest of 1 lemon or lime	
6	5-oz. (150-g) fillets Atlantic salmon	6
2 Tbsp.	minced fresh thyme or lemon thyme	30 mL
1 tsp.	cracked fennel seed	5 mL
	freshly cracked black pepper to taste	
1 tsp.	mustard seed	5 mL
	zest of 1 lemon	
2 Tbsp.	melted honey	30 mL
1 Tbsp.	olive oil	15 mL
1 recipe	Wine Gastrique	1 recipe

To make the brine, combine the wine with the sugar, salt, coriander seed, fennel seed, 2 tsp. (10 mL) mustard seed, peppercorns, bay or lime leaves, ginger, star anise and lemon or lime zest. Boil the mixture long enough to dissolve the sugar and salt, then simmer 10 minutes. Let cool.

Immerse the salmon fillets in the brine in a shallow dish for 15 minutes. If the fish is not completely covered, turn it once or twice. Remove the fish from the brine, pat it dry, and sprinkle the thyme, cracked fennel seed, pepper, 1 tsp. (5 mL) mustard seed and lemon zest on the flesh side. Drizzle the honey and olive oil over the seasonings.

Preheat the oven to 400ºF (200ºC). Place the fish on a shallow baking sheet. Roast until cooked through, 10 to 20 minutes, depending on the thickness of the fish. Place on a serving platter and drizzle with Wine Gastrique.

Wine Gastrique

Makes about 3 Tbsp. (45 mL)

3–4 Tbsp.	white sugar	45–60 mL
½ cup	white wine	120 mL
2–3 Tbsp.	champagne vinegar	30–45 mL
½ tsp.	cracked black peppercorns	2.5 mL
	salt to taste	

In a shallow sauté pan over high heat, caramelize the sugar without stirring, about 3 to 5 minutes. Slowly add the wine and reduce by half its original volume. Add the vinegar and reduce by one-third. Season with pepper and salt to taste.

Prosciutto-Wrapped Ahi Tuna

Ahi tuna (yellowfin) is most often eaten raw in sushi. As this fish has little or no fat, it is imperative not to overcook it or it will become so dry it is barely palatable. The flavour is full and beefy. I like the salty, crispy jacket the prosciutto adds. Even those who claim to not like fish enjoy this as a carnivorous experience. Start this recipe a day ahead so the marmalade has time to set. A garlicky potato and a full-bodied wine are the perfect companions!

— Shelley

Serves 4

1 ½ lbs.	Ahi tuna loin, skinned, about 10 to 12 inches (25 to 30 cm) long	675 g
8	thin, long slices prosciutto (ask for centre cut)	8
3 cups	canola oil	720 mL
3	large parsnips, peeled	3
2 Tbsp.	olive oil	30 mL
	salt and freshly ground black pepper to taste	
1 recipe	Lemon & Blackened Tomato Marmalade	1 recipe

Cut the tuna into 4 pieces of the same size and thickness. Lay 2 prosciutto slices side by side touching each other, put a tuna portion on the prosciutto slices and roll it up. Repeat with the rest of the tuna and prosciutto, then refrigerate until ready to use.

In a large heavy-bottomed pot or deep fryer, heat the canola oil to 375ºF (190ºC). Using a vegetable peeler or mandolin, slice the parsnips into very long, thin strips. Working in small batches, fry the parsnips in the oil until crispy. Remove with a slotted spoon and drain on kitchen towels. Season with salt to taste and set aside.

Preheat a large sauté pan to medium-high and add the olive oil. Season the wrapped tuna portions with salt and pepper and place into the hot pan. Cook the pieces for 30 to 60 seconds on each side so they get evenly browned and crispy, being careful not to overcook. Put some of the marmalade on each plate. Cut each tuna portion into three and arrange on plates. Lay parsnip chips over the tuna and serve.

Lemon & Blackened Tomato Marmalade

This makes a generous amount, so refrigerate the leftovers and serve it with grilled or roast chicken, turkey, ham or pork, with rice dishes, or in sandwiches.

Makes about 12 cups (3 L)

8	lemons, washed	8
7 cups	water	1.7 L
2	bay leaves	2
1 ½ lbs.	sugar	675 g
10	ripe Roma tomatoes	10
½ cup	Niçoise olives, finely chopped	120 mL
½ cup	fresh oregano, chopped	120 mL

Using a vegetable peeler, peel the zest off the lemons in long thin strips. Cut the strips into paper-thin slices. Place the slices into a heavy-bottomed pot and cover with the water. Bring to a boil on high heat, then reduce the heat and simmer for 20 minutes.

Trim away and discard the pith from the lemons. Cut the lemons into quarters lengthwise and then into ¼-inch (.6-cm) slices. Add the lemon slices and bay leaves to the zest in the pot and increase the heat to medium-high, stirring often. When it boils, turn off the heat and let stand 24 hours.

The next day, return the pot to medium heat and add the sugar, stirring to dissolve. Cook at a gentle boil and stir often for 1 to 2 hours or until the mixture begins to thicken.

Cut the Roma tomatoes in half and squeeze out the seeds. Place the tomatoes skin side down on a grill preheated to medium-high. Cook the tomatoes until they are blackened. Add the blackened tomatoes, Niçoise olives and oregano to the lemon mixture. Remove from the heat and let cool.

Grilled Chicken Kebabs with Lemon Rosemary-Basil Marinade

This recipe is easy, versatile and even kid-friendly. You can use chicken breasts left whole or cut to appetizer size, skin on or skinless, bone in or boneless— you get the picture. Rosemary and lemon are a classic combination, but the added basil mellows out the stronger flavoured rosemary and the marinade guarantees your chicken will be moist. Great for summertime barbecuing or winter oven roasting. If you want to prepare the marinade ahead of time, leave out the salt but don't forget to salt the chicken before cooking.

— Karen

Serves 4

1	small onion, quartered	1
½ cup	fresh lemon juice	120 mL
1 Tbsp.	lemon zest	15 mL
2 Tbsp.	fresh rosemary leaves, chopped	30 mL
¼ cup	fresh basil	60 mL
¼ cup	white wine (optional)	60 mL
¼ cup	olive oil	60 mL
1 Tbsp.	sea salt	15 mL
2	chicken breasts, cut into chunks	2

Prepare the marinade by placing the onion, lemon juice, lemon zest, rosemary, basil and white wine in a food processor. Process until fairly smooth, then drizzle in the olive oil and add the salt.

Marinate the chicken pieces in this mixture for at least 30 minutes or up to overnight in the refrigerator. (Do not add salt if leaving overnight.)

Remove the chicken from the marinade and push onto skewers. Grill at medium-high or bake in the oven at 375ºF (190ºC) for about 15 minutes, turning frequently until cooked through.

Chicken Breast Brochettes with Moroccan Chermoula

Serves 6

1 ¼ lbs.	fresh, boneless chicken breasts	565 g
1 tsp.	cumin	5 mL
1 tsp.	paprika	5 mL
½ tsp.	turmeric	2.5 mL
¼ tsp.	cayenne	1.25 mL
2	cloves garlic, minced	2
¼ cup	coarsely grated onion	60 mL
1 tsp.	coarse salt	5 mL
	freshly ground black pepper to taste	
¼ cup	fresh cilantro, chopped	60 mL
¼ cup	fresh parsley, chopped	60 mL
4 Tbsp.	lemon juice	60 mL
3 Tbsp.	extra virgin olive oil	45 mL
12	4- to 5-inch (10- to 12.5-cm) skewers	12

The spicy and piquant chermoula marinade mixture gives the chicken a marvelous flavour. Serve this dish with rice as an entrée or make small brochettes to serve as hors d'oeuvres. Fresh tuna makes a wonderful alternative to the chicken.

— Ellen

Cut the chicken into 1-inch (2.5-cm) cubes and set aside.

To make the chermoula, in a mortar and pestle, blender or food processor, mix together the cumin, paprika, turmeric, cayenne, garlic, onion, salt, pepper, cilantro, parsley, lemon juice, olive oil and 1 Tbsp. (15 mL) water. Pour over the chicken and mix well. Marinate in the refrigerator for 2 hours.

Start your grill or barbecue at medium-high or, if you want to use the oven, preheat the broiler.

Divide the chicken into 12 parts and thread the cubes onto the skewers. Set the skewers on a platter until ready to grill. Reserve the marinade.

Note: The recipe can be prepared to this point 6 hours ahead of serving time.

If you are using a grill, grill the chicken brochettes over a medium-hot fire for 5 to 8 minutes, turning every few minutes and brushing with marinade. If you are using an oven, cook them under the broiler for 5 to 8 minutes, turning every few minutes and brushing with marinade. Remove the brochettes from the heat and place on a platter. Garnish with lemon wedges and serve immediately over saffron rice.

Grilled Chicken Breasts with Roasted Pepper & Olive Relish

This is inspired by Bobby Flay's incredible flavour combinations. Just when we think we've have added enough herbs to the relish, we add more. The relish is a roasted version of salsa—bold, colourful and sweet. The dish looks great served family-style for a summer buffet, and any leftovers can be used for fabulous sandwiches the next day.

— Karen

Serves 6

2 Tbsp.	sherry	30 mL
6 Tbsp.	orange juice	90 mL
1 Tbsp.	New Mexico chili powder	15 mL
6	cloves garlic	6
¼ cup	olive oil	60 mL
3	chicken breasts, halved, boned and skinned	3
1 recipe	Roasted Pepper & Olive Relish	1 recipe

Make a marinade by blending the sherry, orange juice, chili powder and garlic in a blender or food processor until mixed thoroughly. With the motor running, add the olive oil in a stream until the marinade is emulsified. Pour over the chicken breasts and refrigerate, in a covered dish, for at least 1 hour or up to overnight.

Preheat a grill or barbecue to medium. Remove the chicken from the marinade. Grill for 10 minutes on each side, until cooked through. Place the breasts on a platter and pour relish over top. Dig in.

Roasted Pepper & Olive Relish

Makes about 2 cups (480 mL)

2	roasted red and yellow peppers, peeled, seeded and diced (see page 54)	2
1 cup	kalamata olives, pitted	240 mL
1 Tbsp.	garlic, minced	15 mL
¼ cup	fresh thyme leaves	60 mL
¼ cup	fresh parsley leaves, chopped	60 mL
¼ cup	sherry vinegar	60 mL
2 Tbsp.	honey	30 mL
	sea salt and freshly ground black pepper to taste	

Combine all the relish ingredients in a bowl. Season with salt and pepper.

Green Chili Chicken Enchiladas

Serves 6 to 8

1 lb.	boneless chicken breast	450 g
1	bunch green onions, chopped	1
½	bunch cilantro, finely chopped	½
1	7-oz. (200-mL) can chopped green chilies	1
2 cups	sour cream	480 mL
¾ lb.	Monterey jack cheese, grated	340 g
1 tsp.	oregano	5 mL
½ tsp.	chili powder	2.5 mL
1	jalapeño pepper, chopped (optional)	1
1 cup	whipping cream	240 mL
1 cup	light cream	240 mL
12	corn tortillas	12

This is a very rich dish, best served with a green salad and assorted salsas.

— Rosemary

Poach the chicken in water just until cooked, about 10 minutes. Drain and let cool. Cube the chicken and put in a large bowl. Add the green onions, cilantro, green chilies, sour cream, half the grated cheese, oregano, chili powder and jalapeño, if desired.

Preheat the oven to 375ºF (190ºC). Mix the two creams together. Pour just enough cream into a 9- x 13-inch (23- x 33-cm) greased pan to cover the bottom.

Place a generous spoonful of chicken filling into each tortilla middle and roll up, placing in the pan seam side down. The rolls should fit snugly.

Pour the remaining cream over and sprinkle with the remaining cheese. Bake in the oven until bubbly and warm, about 30 to 35 minutes.

Cornish Hen Wrapped in Grape Leaves

*This is dead easy and attractive
enough for any dinner or luncheon party. I like to serve the hens
with a simple rice dish and a
green salad.*

— Ellen

Serves 4

4	small Cornish hens	4
2 Tbsp.	cilantro pesto	30 mL
1	lemon, zest and juice	1
2–3	cloves garlic, chopped	2–3
2–3 Tbsp.	olive oil	30–45 mL
	salt and freshly ground black pepper to taste	
16	bottled grape leaves, rinsed	16

Combine all ingredients except the grape leaves in a glass dish with a cover or in a resealable plastic bag and allow the hens to marinate for 2 or 3 hours in the refrigerator.

Preheat the oven to 400ºF (200ºC). Wrap each bird in 2 to 4 grape leaves without fussing too much. Arrange the birds on a baking sheet and bake for about 25 to 30 minutes, until the chicken is firm and cooked through.

This is a good method for preparing boneless chicken breasts as well, with fewer grape leaves and a shorter cooking time.

Recommended wine:
big fruity Alsatian pinot gris
or French pinot noir

Spicy Stuffed Turkey Breast

Serves 8 to 10

1 lb.	spicy pancetta, finely chopped	450 g
2	small onions, finely chopped	2
1 Tbsp.	garlic, minced	15 mL
1 Tbsp.	fresh Italian parsley, chopped	15 mL
1 Tbsp.	fresh thyme leaves	15 mL
1 Tbsp.	fresh sage leaves, chopped	15 mL
1 cup	bread crumbs, toasted	240 mL
	sea salt and freshly ground black pepper to taste	
1	butterflied whole turkey breast (skin on, boneless, and tenders removed)	1
½ cup	white wine, orange or apple juice	120 mL
1 Tbsp.	unsalted butter	15 mL

To make the stuffing, sauté the pancetta over medium heat until soft. Add the onions and keep stirring until both are beginning to brown, about 10 to 12 minutes altogether. Add the garlic, herbs and bread crumbs. Remove from the heat and season to taste with salt and pepper. Remember, this is a stuffing, so it needs to be quite strong flavoured. Set aside.

Preheat the oven to 400ºF (200ºC). Place the turkey breast skin side down on a clean work surface. Cover the turkey with parchment paper and pound to a thickness of about 1 ¼ inches (3 cm). Spoon the stuffing over the turkey breast and roll up. Tie butcher's string where necessary to hold the roast together. Place in a small roasting pan and add the wine or juice. Bake for about 1 hour until cooked through. Let sit for 10 minutes before carving into slices to serve.

To make a quick gravy, heat the roasting pan on the stovetop and add more liquid to your desired thickness. Reduce, then add the unsalted butter. Strain and season with salt and pepper.

Serve the turkey hot or at room temperature with a fruity chutney spiked with port.

This is **not** a leftover turkey recipe! I had to come up with numerous turkey recipes for a client who was having a Great Canadian turkey fest. The tricky part was that all the food had to be finger food. I did not have the luxury of a dinner plate ready to be smothered with all the trimmings, so every small bite had to be packed with flavour. I adapted this recipe from a stuffing to go under chicken skin before baking. It is not a traditional bready stuffing, but one full of strong flavours and a great, almost crunchy texture.

— Karen

Recommended wine:
soft, fruity New World cabernet
sauvignon, or syrah or zinfandel

Duck Breast in Filo with Shiitake Mushrooms & Red Onion

*Spring and autumn are the sea-
sons when fresh shiitakes are the
most available. Portobello mushrooms are a good substitute, if
shiitakes are not available. Cut
into smaller pieces, these make
wonderful hors d'oeuvres.*

— Judy

Serves 6

3	duck breasts, skin on	3
12 oz.	shiitake mushrooms	340 g
2 Tbsp.	olive oil	30 mL
1	red onion, peeled	1
1 cup	balsamic vinegar	240 mL
¼ tsp.	dried thyme, or 1 tsp. (5 mL) fresh	1.2 mL
¼ tsp.	fresh dried basil, or 1 tsp. (5 mL) fresh	1.2 mL
	salt and freshly ground black pepper to taste	
12 sheets	filo pastry	12 sheets
¼ cup	butter	60 mL
6 cups	mixed greens, washed	1.5 L

Preheat the oven to 350ºF (175ºC). Heat a frying pan on high for a few minutes, then lay the duck breasts in, skin side down. Sear 2 to 3 minutes, until golden brown. Flip over and sear the other side for about 1 minute, then put the breasts in a dish and bake for 8 to 10 minutes for medium-rare, 12 to 15 minutes for medium and 16 to 20 minutes for well done. Set aside.

Toss the shiitake mushrooms in a bowl with 1 Tbsp. (15 mL) olive oil, then place on a hot grill, or sauté in a pan on medium-high. Cook for 3 to 5 minutes and set aside.

Cut the red onion into 6 wedges and toss lightly with the remaining 1 Tbsp. (15 mL) oil. Grill the wedges on a hot grill for 8 to 10 minutes and set aside. The onions will fall apart, but don't worry because everything will eventually go into the same bowl.

Put the balsamic vinegar in a small pot and simmer until the vinegar is half the original volume.

Meanwhile, slice the duck into short, thin strips and place in a large bowl. Slice the shiitakes into thin strips and add them to the bowl, then add the red onions. Finally, add the herbs, salt and pepper, stir everything together and set to one side.

Preheat the oven to 350°F (175°C). Lay one sheet of filo on a cutting board so the long side is parallel with the edge of the table. Keep the other sheets covered with a damp towel until they are needed. Melt the butter in a pan and brush lightly over the whole sheet. Then add a second sheet of filo and brush it with butter.

Divide the duck mixture into 6 equal portions. Take one portion and spread it along the edge of the filo closest to you, leaving a margin of 1 inch (2.5 cm). Fold in the left and right side of the filo, then fold the edge closest to you over the mixture and carefully roll up the sheet, rolling away from yourself. Place the roll seam down on a baking sheet lined with parchment paper.

Repeat these steps with the remaining filo and duck mixture until you have all six rolls on the tray.

With a serrated knife, make three small cuts at a slight angle on top of each roll to divide it into three. Bake for 12 to 15 minutes, until they are lightly browned.

Remove from the oven and cut into three portions, following the serrated lines. Arrange the pieces on a bed of mixed greens and serve.

Brome Lake Duck Breast en façon de Mme Kamman

Duck, yum yum. My favourite. If you don't share my passion for quackers, use chicken breasts, but it won't be the same, not even close. . . . This dish was inspired by my mentor, Madeleine Kamman, French-American autocrat and matriarch of the culinary world. It clearly illustrates her passion for quality and attention to methodology—and my favourite flavours. Duck and cherries is a classic that just needs a new approach to be relevant again.

I served this with roasted fennel, spinach with pancetta and garlic, potatoes "Anna" and roasted sweet bell peppers at a food and wine weekend in the Canadian Rockies one winter.

— dee

Serves 4

¼ cup	dried sour cherries	60 mL
2	whole star anise	2
½ cup	red wine	120 mL
	zest of 1 lemon	
2	large boneless duck breasts, skin on	2
½ tsp.	ground star anise	2.5 mL
1 tsp.	finely grated ginger root	5 mL
1 tsp.	finely grated orange or tangerine zest	5 mL
1 tsp.	finely minced fresh thyme	5 mL
	freshly cracked black pepper	
1 tsp.	olive oil	5 mL
2	shallots, minced	2
2 tsp.	grated ginger root	10 mL
1 tsp.	olive oil	5 mL
½ cup	red wine	120 mL
½ cup	veal stock	120 mL
½ cup	whipping cream	120 mL
	salt and freshly ground black pepper to taste	
	lemon juice to taste	
	minced chives, for garnish	

Rehydrate the cherries in a small pot with the whole star anise and $1/2$ cup (120 mL) red wine. Simmer to reduce the wine to a syrup, pick out the whole star anise and discard. Set the cherries aside.

In a small pot, put the zest in $1/2$ cup (120 mL) cold water and bring to a boil. Drain and rinse. Repeat twice and set aside.

Cut the whole breasts in half lengthwise. Trim each by removing most of the fat, leaving only a centre strip about $1/2$ inch (1.2 cm) wide running the length of each half breast.

Prepare a rub by mixing together the ground star anise, ginger, orange or tangerine zest, thyme, pepper and 1 tsp. (5 mL) oil. Smear the rub on the breasts. Cover loosely and chill, removing the meat from the fridge 10 to 20 minutes before cooking to take off the chill.

Heat a sauté pan over medium-high until sizzling, add a little olive oil and cook the duck breasts to medium-done, about 10 minutes. Remove from the heat and sprinkle with salt to taste. Let stand 10 minutes.

Sauté the shallots and ginger in 1 tsp. (5 mL) oil until tender and transparent. Add $1/2$ cup (120 mL) red wine. Reduce by half. Add the stock and reduce by half. Add the cream and reduce by half again. Stir in the reserved cherries and lemon zest, then balance to taste with salt, pepper and lemon juice.

To serve, slice the breast on an angle. Drizzle individual serving plates with 1 to 2 Tbsp. (15 to 30 mL) of sauce, then top with the sliced duck. Garnish each plate with several cherries and a sprinkle of lemon zest, and scatter minced chives over top.

Duck Magret with Port Sauce & Rapini

Serves 2

2	shallots, finely diced	2
1 Tbsp.	olive oil	15 mL
2 cups	chicken stock	480 mL
6 oz.	dried figs, quartered	170 g
1 cup	cabernet sauvignon	240 mL
½ cup	port	120 mL
	salt and freshly ground black pepper to taste	
1 ¼ lbs.	rapini, washed and tough ends trimmed	565 g
1	1-lb. (450-g) duck magret	1
3	cloves garlic, peeled and thinly sliced	3

Sauté the shallots in the olive oil over medium heat without browning. Add the stock and boil to reduce by half. Add the figs and cabernet and reduce by half again. Finish with the port. Season to taste with salt and pepper. Keep warm.

While the sauce is reducing, bring a large pot of salted water to a boil. Blanch the rapini until the ends are tender, about 3 to 5 minutes. Drain.

Preheat the oven to 400°F (200°C). Heat a cast-iron frying pan over high heat to smoking hot. With a sharp knife, score the duck skin in a crosshatch pattern. Sear the breast, fat side down, for 4 to 5 minutes to crisp the skin and render the fat. Turn and sear the other side for 2 to 3 minutes, then turn skin side down again to continue rendering. Pour off some of the duck fat into a sauté pan for sautéeing the rapini. Transfer the duck in the cast-iron pan to the oven to finish cooking for another 4 to 5 minutes.

Add the garlic to the duck fat in the sauté pan. Cook the garlic over medium heat for 4 to 5 minutes without browning, then add the rapini and sauté long enough to heat through. Season to taste with salt and pepper.

Remove the duck from the oven; it should be medium-rare. Slice diagonally. Spoon port sauce onto 2 serving plates and arrange the duck on top. Serve with the rapini on the side.

Spicy Cowboy Steak & Beer-Battered Onion Rings

Serves 4

4	striploin steaks, about 8 oz. (225 g) each	4
1 recipe	Onion Rings (see page 96)	1 recipe

For the rub:

2 Tbsp.	coarsely cracked black peppercorns	30 mL
2 tsp.	onion powder	10 mL
2 tsp.	granulated garlic	10 mL
2 tsp.	paprika	10 mL
1 tsp.	chili powder	5 mL
2 Tbsp.	Dijon mustard	30 mL
1 Tbsp.	olive oil	15 mL

Combine the rub ingredients to form a thick paste and slather over both sides of the steaks. Marinate in a shallow dish or a sealed plastic bag in the refrigerator for 2 hours.

Heat the barbecue to medium-high. Cook the steaks for 4 to 5 minutes on each side, until just medium-rare.

Serve the steaks topped with a pile of hot onion rings.

A grilled steak topped with onion rings is classic steakhouse fare. These onions have a crispy beer batter that I make with local Big Rock ale, an Alberta brew. You can use your favourite microbrewed pale ale. Gild the lily by serving your spicy steak with a pile of garlic- or horseradish-spiked mashed potatoes.

— Cinda

Steak Touch Test

Wonder when your steak is done to your liking?

Use the steakhouse chef touch test—something I learned from someone used to cranking out dozens of red meat meals at a Calgary steakhouse. I call it the steakhouse "rule of thumb." If you know how a steak feels when it's done, you'll never be stuck with over-or undercooked meat again.

• Relax your hand and press the triangle of flesh below your thumb. That's how a spongy rare steak feels.

• Holding your thumb and index finger together, press the spot again. It's firmer, like a steak that's cooked medium-rare.

• When you touch your thumb and middle finger together, the spot gets even firmer, like a steak that's cooked to medium or medium-well.

• Your thumb and fourth finger are bouncy, like a steak that's tough and well done. If you go any further, that steak is shoe leather!

— Cinda Chavich

Onion Rings

Serves 4

1 cup	all-purpose flour	240 mL
½ cup	whole wheat flour	120 mL
1 tsp.	paprika	5 mL
½ tsp.	salt	2.5 mL
1	bottle pale ale	1
1	egg	1
1 Tbsp.	canola oil	15 mL
2	medium white onions, peeled	2
	canola oil for frying	
	salt to taste	

To make the batter for the onions, combine the flours, paprika and salt. Beat in the ale, egg and 1 Tbsp. (15 mL) oil until smooth. Let the batter stand for 2 hours in the refrigerator.

Slice the onions into ⅛-inch (.25-cm) rounds, discarding the centres, and separate into rings.

Heat 2 to 3 inches (5 to 7.5 cm) of canola oil in a deep, heavy skillet or wok. The oil must be hot, about 350°F (175°C), but watch it carefully. The oil is hot enough when a cube of bread browns in about 25 seconds.

Using a fork, quickly dip the onion rings in the batter and shake off any excess. Deep-fry the rings in hot oil in batches for about 1 minute, until golden and crisp. Drain on paper towels, sprinkle with salt and keep warm in a low oven. Reheat the oil between batches and continue until all the onions are cooked.

mango & duck salad with tangerine dressing (page 48)

grilled portobello & yam terrine with bleu de causse (page 148)

pasta with lavender-cream vegetable medley sauce (page 123)

chocolate espresso milkshake (page 184)
and baci di cioccolati (page 207)

Recommended wine:
southern French blend (try languedoc—
syrah/grenache/mourvedre)

Beef Tenderloin with Shallot & Herb Confit

Serves 4

1 ½ lbs.	beef tenderloin, centre cut	675 g
4	shallots, chopped fine	4
1 Tbsp.	capers, drained and chopped fine	15 mL
½ cup	fresh herbs, chopped fine	120 mL
1 Tbsp.	olive oil	15 mL
	sea salt and freshly ground black pepper to taste	

Have the butcher butterfly the beef lengthwise or use a long, sharp slicing knife to slice into the beef so that the cut portion is about ¾ inch (2 cm) thick. Keep slicing sideways, holding the knife flat. If you hold the uncut portion of beef, it is easier to keep the thickness of the cut portion even. When you reach the end, flatten out the meat into a rectangle.

Mix together the shallots, capers and herbs and place them on the meat. Roll the beef up evenly lengthwise and tie it at regular intervals with butcher's string. The beef can be prepared 1 hour before or up to 24 hours ahead, if you wrap it and set it in the refrigerator.

Preheat the oven to 350°F (175°C). Spread the olive oil over the beef and season with salt and pepper. The best way to cook the beef is to sear it on all sides in a hot cast-iron pan, then roast it in the oven for 15 minutes. It can also be grilled on the barbecue over medium heat, turning to cook evenly on all sides.

Let the meat sit for at least 5 minutes before carving into medallions.

Beef tenderloin is the most wonderful meat because it's tender, cooks quickly and you can infuse it with just about any flavour you want. In the summertime, try this recipe using only fresh herbs such as basil, chives, chervil and parsley. The contrast of the crisp exterior and the buttery smooth flavour tastes great at any temperature.

— Karen

Tenderloin for Two with Blue Cheese Butter

*Sometimes you need
something tasty and simple
for a special dinner for you
and your significant other.
Too much fussing ruins the
mood—that's when a steak
and compound butter hits
the mark. Pour your favourite
hearty red wine, start a fire
and relax. Steamed baby
vegetables and roasted or
garlic mashed potatoes
make the perfect, worry-
free accompaniments.*

— Cinda

Serves 2

2	6-oz. (170-g) beef tenderloin steaks, about 1 ½ inches (4 cm) thick	2
1 tsp.	Worcestershire sauce	5 mL
1 Tbsp.	black peppercorns, coarsely crushed	15 mL
2 Tbsp.	olive oil	30 mL
¼ recipe	Blue Cheese Butter	¼ recipe

Rub the steaks with Worcestershire and press crushed peppercorns onto both sides. Heat the oil in a heavy, non-stick pan over high heat. When the pan is very hot, add the steaks. Sauté for 4 minutes per side for medium-rare.

Transfer to serving plates and top each steak with a dollop of blue cheese butter on top. Serve immediately.

Blue Cheese Butter

*This recipe makes enough butter for several steaks. You can freeze
the extra in logs, and slice off coins to top your next steaks. Just
spoon the butter along one edge of a piece of plastic wrap, then
roll into a log, twisting the ends to seal.*

Makes about ½ cup (120 mL)

¼ cup	unsalted butter, softened	60 mL
3 Tbsp.	crumbled Roquefort or other blue cheese	45 mL
2 Tbsp.	chopped chives	30 mL
1 tsp.	fresh lemon juice	5 mL
dash	cognac	dash

Beat the butter until light and fluffy. Beat in the cheese, chives, lemon juice and cognac. Set aside.

Recommended wine:
big red with backbone (try California
cabernet sauvignon or Meritage)

Grilled Beef Tenderloin with Heart-Stopping Roquefort Sauce

Serves 8

1 ½ lbs.	beef tenderloin (trimmed of any extra fat)	680 g
2	French baguettes, sliced on the bias into ½-inch (1-cm) slices	2
2 cups	fresh, washed arugula or spinach, larger pieces torn	480 mL
1 recipe	Heart-Stopping Roquefort Sauce	1 recipe

Preheat the grill to medium-high. Grill the tenderloin to medium-rare and allow it to rest for 5 to 10 minutes. Thinly slice the tenderloin and arrange on a platter. Serve the beef, sliced bread, greens and sauce "fresco style."

This is a great casual entertaining entrée for buffet-style dining. The leftover sauce can be turned into a delicious salad dressing over mixed greens, garnished with some lightly toasted walnuts and perhaps some of the remaining tenderloin. Allow ¼ pound (115 g) beef tenderloin per person for a luncheon, and somewhat more for dinner.

— Janet

Heart-Stopping Roquefort Sauce

Makes 1 ½ cups (360 mL)

¾ cup	dry white wine	180 mL
1 cup	whipping cream	240 mL
¼ lb.	Roquefort cheese, softened	115 g
½ cup	unsalted butter, softened	120 mL
	white pepper to taste	

In a small saucepan, reduce the wine over moderate heat to 1 Tbsp. (15 mL). Add the cream and reduce by half over moderate heat.

Combine the cheese and butter until smooth. Whisk the cheese mixture into the wine mixture a little at a time until it is incorporated. Simmer the sauce for 5 minutes on low, whisking to prevent sticking. Strain the sauce through a fine sieve into a serving bowl. Add white pepper to taste.

Filo Beef Wellington with Roasted Shallot Demi-Glaze

Although I had the displeasure of witnessing how "foie gras" is made while I was at school in France, I still love the flavour. You can use the duxelle, your favourite pâté or the foie gras for this recipe. The special thing about this dish is that it presents a lovely gift for each dinner guest.

— Judy

Serves 6

6	4-oz. (115-g) beef fillets	6
1 Tbsp.	olive oil	15 mL
6 sheets	filo pastry	6 sheets
¼ cup	butter	60 mL
1 recipe	Duxelle or 12 oz. (340 g) pâté de foie gras	1 recipe
1 recipe	Roasted Shallot Demi-Glaze	1 recipe

Rub the fillets all over with the oil. Preheat a frying pan over medium-high. Place the fillet in the pan and sear until lightly browned, about 2 minutes per side. Set aside.

Preheat the oven to 350°F (175°C). Lay one sheet of filo on a cutting board so the long side is parallel with the edge of the table. Keep the other sheets covered with a damp towel until they are needed. Melt the butter in a pan and brush lightly over the sheet. Then add a second sheet of filo and brush it with butter.

Cut the filo in two pieces. Take one fillet and place it along the edge of the filo closest to you, leaving a margin of 1 inch (2.5 cm). Spread ⅙ of the Duxelle all over the fillet. Fold in the left and right sides of the filo, then fold the edge closest to you over the fillet and carefully roll up the sheet, rolling away from yourself. Place the roll seam down on a baking sheet lined with parchment paper.

Repeat these steps with the remaining filo and fillets until you have all six rolls on the tray.

Bake for 10 to 15 minutes, until the rolls are lightly browned.

Arrange the Wellingtons on individual plates and spoon the demi-glaze around each bundle. Serve immediately.

Duxelle

Makes 1 ½ cups (360 mL)

2 Tbsp.	butter	30 mL
1 lb.	mushrooms, washed and finely chopped	450 g
3	shallots, peeled and finely chopped	3
	salt and freshly ground black pepper to taste	

Heat a frying pan over medium-high. Add the butter, mushrooms and shallots and cook until all the liquid has disappeared, 5 to 10 minutes. Season with salt and pepper to taste.

Roasted Shallot Demi-Glaze

Makes 1 ½ cups (360 mL)

9	shallots, peeled and cut in half	9
2 Tbsp.	olive oil	30 mL
1 cup	balsamic vinegar	240 mL
3 cups	beef stock	720 mL
¼ tsp.	thyme	1.2 mL
	salt and freshly ground black pepper to taste	

Preheat the oven to 375°F (190°C). Rub the shallots with the oil and bake for 25 minutes. Place them in a saucepan and add the balsamic vinegar. Reduce until there is only a tablespoon (15 mL) of liquid left. Add the stock and reduce by half. Add the thyme, then season with the salt and pepper. Serve hot.

Oven-Braised Beef Stew with Double-Smoked Bacon and Red Pepper & Sage Biscuits

This stew was inspired by the wonderful double-smoked bacon found at Alberta farmers' markets. It's layered and slowly braised, like a traditional French daube—but remember you'll have to start the meat marinating the night before. Serve this tender stew with these flavourful biscuits or with a pile of mashed Yukon Gold potatoes.

— Cinda

Serves 6

3 lbs.	lean stewing beef cut into 2-inch (5-cm) cubes	1.3 kg
1 ½ cups	dry red wine	360 mL
¼ cup	rye whisky	60 mL
2 Tbsp.	olive oil	30 mL
2 tsp.	salt	10 mL
½ tsp.	freshly ground black pepper	2.5 mL
1 tsp.	thyme or sage	5 mL
1	bay leaf, crumbled	1
2	cloves garlic, minced	2
2 cups	thinly sliced white onions	480 mL
2 cups	sliced carrots	480 mL
½ lb.	lean, double-smoked bacon, sliced, then cut into 2-inch (5-cm) strips	225 g
2 cups	sliced fresh mushrooms (a mixture of white, brown, oyster and wild mushrooms)	480 mL
2 cups	canned Roma tomatoes, chopped or puréed	480 mL
1 cup	flour	240 mL
2 cups	beef stock or bouillon	480 mL
1 recipe	Red Pepper & Sage Biscuits	1 recipe

In a glass bowl or resealable plastic bag, combine the beef cubes, wine, whisky, olive oil, salt, pepper, thyme or sage, bay leaf, garlic, onions and carrots. Refrigerate overnight.

The next day, bring the meat and vegetables to room temperature. Simmer the bacon in boiling water for 10 minutes, then drain and pat dry. Slice the mushrooms and chop the tomatoes.

Drain the beef and vegetables, reserving the marinade. Line the bottom of a deep ovenproof casserole dish with a few strips of bacon. Add a handful of marinated onion and carrot, then some of the mushrooms and chopped tomatoes.

Roll each piece of beef in flour and arrange some of the meat in a single layer on top. Cover with more bacon and vegetables, then another layer of floured beef. Continue in this manner, ending with a layer of vegetables, then bacon on top.

Pour in the reserved marinade and enough beef stock to almost cover the meat and vegetables. Bring to a boil on top of the stove, then cover tightly and place the casserole in a 325°F (165°C) oven. Braise the stew for 3 to 4 hours, until everything is very tender. Serve with Red Pepper & Sage Biscuits.

Red Pepper & Sage Biscuits

Home-roasted peppers are wonderful, but if you are short on time, use commercially roasted peppers from a jar. Drain them well and pat dry before chopping them and mixing into the biscuit dough.

Makes 10 to 12

1 cup	all-purpose flour	240 mL
1 cup	whole wheat flour	240 mL
pinch	sugar	pinch
½ tsp.	salt	2.5 mL
2 Tbsp.	baking powder	30 mL
½ cup	unsalted butter, cold	120 mL
1	red bell pepper, roasted, peeled and chopped (see page 54), about 1 cup (240 mL)	1
2 Tbsp.	chopped fresh sage	30 mL
½ cup	half-and-half cream	120 mL

Combine the flours with the sugar, salt and baking powder in a large bowl. Cut the butter into small cubes and, using your fingers or a pastry blender, work the butter into the flour until the mixture resembles coarse crumbs.

Chop the red pepper into small pieces and mix into the dough along with the sage.

Add enough cream to make a soft dough. Transfer to a floured surface and knead very lightly, just a few turns, then pat into a thick round, about 1 1/2 inches (4 cm) thick.

Preheat the oven to 425°F (220°C). Using a large glass or cutter, cut into biscuits about 2 to 3 inches (5 to 7.5 cm) in diameter. Place on a baking sheet lined with parchment paper and bake for about 15 minutes, until lightly golden. Serve warm with butter.

Big Rock Beef Ragout

Beef stew can be made any time of the year, but I find that fall yields the best choice of vegetables to add to the pot. I always use onions, potatoes and carrots. But depending on what is available, I may add any of the following: turnips, parsnips, tomatoes, fennel, green beans or squash. Let your taste be your guide.

Since moving to Calgary, I've become a fan of Big Rock Brewery, a local company, and I like to use Big Rock Black Amber Ale in this dish. Any dark stout or ale will work, however, to add a wonderful richness.

— Rosemary

Serves 6 to 8

2 ½ lbs.	boneless beef roast, cubed	1 kg
3 Tbsp.	flour	45 mL
2 Tbsp.	olive oil	30 mL
2	onions, chopped	2
2	carrots, peeled and chopped	2
1–2 lbs.	any other vegetables	450–900 g
3	cloves garlic, minced	3
½ cup	red wine	120 mL
1	bottle dark beer or stout	1
3 cups	beef stock	720 mL
1 lb.	baby red potatoes, whole	450 g
1–2 Tbsp.	fresh herbs (thyme, oregano, basil)	15–30 mL
	salt and freshly ground black pepper to taste	

Roll the beef cubes in the flour. In a large, heavy casserole or deep roasting pan, heat the oil over medium-high. Brown the meat on all sides, for 5 to 10 minutes in all. Remove from the pan.

In the same pan, sauté the onion, carrots and any other hard root vegetable for 5 minutes. Add the garlic and cook for 1 minute. Add the wine and scrape down the sides and bottom of the pan. Add the beef, beer, stock and potatoes. The amount of stock needed may vary depending on the amount and type of vegetables. The key is to just cover everything while the stew is simmering.

Cook for 1 hour, covered, at a simmer. Add any other vegetables and cook another 1 ½ to 2 hours or more, until the beef is tender. Add the fresh herbs and salt and pepper.

Let the stew sit for 20 minutes before serving. For a finishing touch, garnish with sprigs of fresh herbs.

Osso Buco

Serves 4 to 6

6 Tbsp.	olive oil	90 mL
6	veal shanks with bone and marrow intact, 1 ¹/₂ inches (3.8 cm) thick	6
¼ cup	flour	60 mL
1	medium onion, sliced	1
2–3	medium carrots, chopped	2–3
1	celery stalk, chopped	1
1	14-oz. (398-mL) can plum tomatoes	1
1 Tbsp.	tomato paste	15 mL
½ cup	white wine	120 mL
½ cup	chicken stock	120 mL
	generous pinch of saffron	
	salt and pepper to taste	
	dried Seville orange peel	
1 recipe	Gremolata	1 recipe

This is a classic treatment of an Italian favourite with the addition of carrots and saffron. I love their flavour combined with the punch of the gremolata. When I make Seville marmalade in January or February, I zest several Seville oranges with a potato peeler and dry the peel to use in any number of stews or soups. Use ordinary orange peel (the zest only) as a substitute.

— Ellen

Heat the oil over medium-high in a large, heavy-bottomed pan. Dredge the veal shanks in flour and fry on both sides until well browned. Remove to a plate. Add the onion, carrot and celery to the remaining oil in the pan and sauté until soft.

Stir in the tomatoes, tomato paste, wine, stock, saffron, salt and pepper, and orange peel. Bring to a boil, add the browned veal, lower the heat to simmer and cover. Simmer gently until tender, 1 ¹/₂ to 2 hours.

Gremolata

²/₃ cup	finely chopped Italian parsley	160 mL
2	cloves garlic, minced	2
	zest of 1 lemon	

Combine the ingredients well. Sprinkle the Gremolata over the Osso Buco. Serve with a simple creamy risotto.

Chili-Glazed Baby Back Ribs

*This is the perfect way to create
tender, flavourful ribs on the grill.
Don't succumb to the theory that
ribs need to be preboiled to be
tender. Start with baby back ribs
(far more succulent than the less
expensive side ribs) and don't forget to remove the skin from the
back of the rack, and you'll have
tender ribs every time. To remove
the membrane, peel the silvery
skin off the back side of the racks.
(Free a corner of the skin, then
grab it with a paper towel for
grip and pull it off in one piece.)*

— Cinda

Serves 4

4	dried ancho chilies (see page 107)	4
2	cloves garlic, pressed	2
½ tsp.	oregano	2.5 mL
½ tsp.	cocoa powder	2.5 mL
¼ tsp.	cinnamon	1 mL
¼ tsp.	cumin	1 mL
2 Tbsp.	apple cider vinegar	30 mL
½ cup	dark beer	120 mL
½ tsp.	salt	2.5 mL
3 Tbsp.	tomato paste	45 mL
3 Tbsp.	dark honey or maple syrup	45 mL
4 lbs.	baby back ribs, silvery skin peeled off the back of each rack	2 kg

In a hot, dry cast-iron pan, toast the chilies on each side for about 20 seconds, pressing down with a spatula. The chilies should just begin to soften and become fragrant, not scorch. Place them in a bowl of very hot water to rehydrate for 20 minutes.

When the chilies are soft, drain off the water, remove the stems and seeds and place the chilies in a food processor or blender with the garlic, oregano, cocoa, cinnamon, cumin, vinegar and beer. Process until smooth. Add the salt and tomato paste and whirl to combine. Divide the marinade in half.

Combine half of the marinade with the honey or maple syrup and refrigerate for use while grilling. Use the remaining marinade on the ribs, rubbing it well into all surfaces of the meat. Cover the ribs and refrigerate overnight.

Before cooking, bring the meat to room temperature. Heat one side of the barbecue to medium. Grill the ribs over medium indirect heat, placing them on the unlit side of the grill with a drip pan underneath. Cover the barbecue and cook the ribs for 1 hour, brushing heavily with the remaining marinade during the last 15 minutes only, to prevent the sauce from burning.

Madame Simone's Milanese Pork Chops

Serves 4

1 Tbsp.	olive oil	15 mL
4	thick pork loin chops	4
½	lemon, juice only	½
2	cloves garlic, finely chopped	2
2 Tbsp.	fresh rosemary, roughly chopped	30 mL
	sea salt and freshly ground black pepper to taste	

In a heavy-bottomed frying pan over medium-high, sear the pork chops in the olive oil briefly on both sides. Reduce the heat to a simmer, add the remaining ingredients and cover. Cook for approximately 15 minutes. Cooking the meat slowly is the secret to this tender and simply delicious dish.

When my dear friend, the mezzo soprano Heather Meyers, was apprenticing at La Scala in Milan a few years ago, a wizened old woman, four feet tall with one black eyebrow, insisted she learn to cook "carne" properly. What follows is Madame Simone's recipe.

— Rhondda

Ancho Chilies

Ancho chilies are dried poblaño peppers—a heart-shaped, deep burgundy chili pepper with a rich, almost raisinlike sweetness and mild to medium degree of heat.

Toasting chilies in a hot skillet before rehydrating them intensifies the flavours. Use a spatula to press the dry chili onto the hot surface until it loses its crispy texture and becomes pliable, but be careful not to burn it. It only takes a few seconds over fairly high heat.

Look for dried ancho chilies in the produce section of the supermarket or in a Latin or Mexican food store. You can substitute the longer, pasilla chili—they are slightly hotter—if you can't find an ancho, although the flavour will be a little different.

— Cinda Chavich

Pork & Sweet Potato Pot Pie

This is the kind of dish to enjoy on a winter evening—the sweet potatoes and cilantro add a jolt of colour to this tender pork stew. If you don't want to make the biscuits, the stew is also tasty served over rice.

— Cinda

Serves 6

2 Tbsp.	olive oil	15 mL
3 lbs.	boneless pork shoulder, well trimmed of fat and cut into 2-inch (5-cm) cubes	1.4 kg
1	large white onion, chopped	1
1 lb.	sweet potatoes, peeled and cubed	450 g
3 Tbsp.	flour	45 mL
2 cups	chicken stock, preferably homemade	480 mL
1 cup	white wine	240 mL
2 Tbsp.	balsamic vinegar	30 mL
5	cloves garlic, minced	5
2 tsp.	ground cumin	10 mL
¼ tsp.	cayenne pepper	1 mL
¼ tsp.	freshly ground black pepper	1 mL
½ cup	chopped cilantro	120 mL
1 recipe	Cheese Biscuit Crust	1 recipe
	paprika, for dusting	

In a large Dutch oven, heat the oil and cook the pork cubes in batches over medium-high heat for 5 to 10 minutes, until nicely browned on all sides. Remove the meat and set aside as it browns, adding more pork cubes to the pan.

When all the meat is browned, add the onion and sweet potato to the pan and cook over medium-high heat until both just begin to brown and caramelize, about 5 to 10 minutes. Add the flour and stir to coat, then slowly add the stock and wine. Bring the mixture to a boil, stirring up any browned bits on the bottom of the pan, then add the vinegar, garlic, cumin, cayenne and pepper. Return the browned pork cubes to the pot, stir, cover and turn the heat down to low.

Simmer the stew for 1 hour, stirring occasionally to make sure it doesn't stick. Prepare the Cheese Biscuit Crust while the stew simmers.

When the stew is cooked and the pork is tender, stir in the chopped cilantro. Preheat the oven to 400°F (200°C). Pour the stew into an oval baking dish that you can take to the table, and drop the biscuit mixture on top by spoonfuls to rustically cover the meat.

Bake for 25 to 30 minutes, until the biscuit topping is golden and the pie is bubbling. Dust with paprika before serving.

Cheese Biscuit Crust

½ cup	all-purpose flour	240 mL
½ cup	whole wheat flour	240 mL
½ tsp.	salt	2.5 mL
1 tsp.	baking powder	5 mL
2 Tbsp.	cold butter	30 mL
1 cup	grated white cheddar	240 mL
⅔ cup	skim milk	160 mL

Combine the flours, salt and baking powder in a bowl.
Using a pastry blender, cut in the cold butter until the
mixture resembles coarse crumbs. Stir in the grated
cheese and enough of the milk to make a soft dough.
(You may not need to use all of the milk.)

Mexican Green Chili Pork Stew (Chile Verde)

Gail and I discovered this great
dish on a trip to New Mexico
some years ago and we've been
making a variation of it ever since.
Try adding a can of drained white
hominy corn for an authentic
touch and interesting texture.

— Ellen

Serves 6 to 8

6–8	tomatillos	6–8
3 lbs.	boneless pork, trimmed and cut into 1-inch (2.5-cm) cubes	1.35 kg
½ cup	flour	120 mL
4 Tbsp.	olive oil	60 mL
2 cups	onion, chopped	480 mL
½ cup	celery, chopped	120 mL
1 Tbsp.	minced garlic	15 mL
2	minced jalapeños	2
6 cups	rich stock	1.5 L
1	27-oz. (765-mL) can diced green chilies	1
1	14-oz. (398-mL) can creamed corn	1
¼ cup	minced cilantro	60 mL
2 tsp.	minced fresh oregano	10 mL
1–2	ripe avocadoes	1–2

Cover the tomatillos with water in a saucepan and boil over medium heat for 5 minutes. Drain, rinse and drain again. Chop coarsely and set aside.

Dredge the pork cubes in the flour. In a heavy Dutch oven on medium-high heat, heat 2 Tbsp. (30 mL) olive oil and cook the pork (in batches if necessary) until browned. Set the meat aside.

Heat the remaining 2 Tbsp. (30 mL) oil in the same pot and sauté the onions, celery, garlic, chopped tomatillos and jalapeños until the onions are soft, 5 to 10 minutes. Add the pork to the pot. Add the stock, green chilies, corn, cilantro and oregano and bring to a boil, carefully scraping up bits from the bottom.

Lower the heat and simmer, covered, until the meat is tender (45 minutes to 1 hour). Add more stock (or beer, if you wish), if needed as the liquid reduces.

Stir in coarsely mashed avocado just before serving. Serve with cornbread and a salad.

Cassoulet with Sausage & Smoked Pork Hock

Serves 8 to 10 friends generously

2	onions, thickly diced	2
2	leeks, coarsely chopped	2
2	carrots, coarsely chopped	2
2	celery stalks, coarsely chopped	2
8	cloves garlic, sliced	8
1 Tbsp.	olive oil	15 mL
2	links spicy Italian sausage, sliced	2
2	bay leaves	2
2–3	sprigs fresh rosemary	2–3
4–5	sprigs fresh thyme	4–5
2–3	sprigs fresh sage	2–3
1 tsp.	dried oregano	5 mL
1 tsp.	dried basil	5 mL
1 or 2	whole star anise	1 or 2
½	stick cinnamon, broken	¹/₂
1 Tbsp.	cracked peppercorns	15 mL
½ tsp.	cracked allspice berries	2.5 mL
4–6	whole cloves	4–6
	zest of 1 lemon	
1 cup	red wine	240 mL
½ cup	pomegranate molasses	120 mL
4 cups	raw green lentils	1 L
1	smoked pork hock, whole	1
8 cups	chicken or beef stock	2 L
	kosher salt and freshly ground black pepper to taste	
1–2 Tbsp.	herb-infused wine vinegar	15–30 mL

Rustic food that simmers untended all afternoon is a wonderful restorative. Serve this hearty dish with simple greens, crusty bread, wine and a great deal of passion for the simple things of life.

— dee

Over medium heat in a heavy-bottomed, ovenproof brazier, cook the onions, leeks, carrots, celery and garlic in the olive oil, adding small amounts of water as needed to prevent browning. Once the vegetables are tender, 10 to 15 minutes, allow the water to evaporate and the vegetables to brown for colour and flavour.

Add the sausage, herbs and spices, lemon zest, wine, molasses, lentils, pork hock and stock. Stir well, bring to a boil, then cover snugly and pop into the oven at 375ºF (190ºC) for 3 hours. Add more water or stock if the level of liquid drops below the tops of the food.

Skim any fat from the surface, and add salt, pepper and a splash of vinegar to taste. Skin the pork hock and shred the meat, discarding the skin and bones. Serve generous portions.

Venison Chili with Black Beans & Rye Whisky

If venison is not available, substitute beef chuck steak or stew meat. In the Italian sausage department, the Calgary-made Spolumbo's spicy Italian is my favourite for fresh, lean pork sausage.

— Cinda

Serves 8

2	dried ancho chilies (see page 107)	2
3 Tbsp.	canola oil	45 mL
1 ½ lbs.	venison shoulder (or beef chuck steak), cut into ¼-inch (.6-cm) cubes	675 g
1	large yellow onion, chopped	1
4	cloves garlic, minced	4
¼ lb.	spicy Italian sausage	100 g
2 tsp.	ground cumin	10 mL
1 tsp.	cayenne pepper	5 mL
2	19-oz. (532-mL) cans Roma tomatoes,chopped or whirled in a food processor to break up	2
¼ cup	rye whisky	60 mL
2 tsp.	dried oregano	10 mL
1 ½ cups	cooked black beans (see page 154)	360 mL
¼ cup	tomato paste	60 mL
2 Tbsp.	brown sugar or maple syrup	30 mL
	salt and freshly ground black pepper to taste	

Toast the chilies in a hot, dry cast-iron pan for 20 seconds a side, pressing with a spatula to soften. Soak the toasted chilies in a bowl of very hot water for 20 minutes to rehydrate. Drain. Discard the stems and seeds and chop the chilies.

In a large Dutch oven, heat the oil over medium-high heat and brown the venison or beef in batches, about 10 minutes for each batch. Remove it to a plate using a slotted spoon and set aside. It should be nicely caramelized—if the meat is stewing in its own juice, the pan is overcrowded and not hot enough.

When the meat is all browned and has been set aside, add the onion and garlic to the pan. Remove the sausage from its casing and crumble into the pan. Cook until the sausage is no longer pink and the onion is soft. Stir in the chopped ancho chilies, cumin and cayenne and cook for 2 minutes.

Return the venison or beef to the pan and add the tomatoes, whisky and oregano. Bring to a boil, reduce the heat to low, cover the pot and simmer the chili for 1 ½ hours.

When the meat is tender, add the black beans, tomato paste and brown sugar or maple syrup. Stir to combine well and simmer 15 minutes longer. Season to taste with salt and pepper.

Grilled Lamb, Pork or Beef with Assyrian Marinade

Serves 6

1	large onion	1
2–3	cloves garlic	2–3
1 tsp.	dried basil	5 mL
1 tsp.	parsley	5 mL
½ cup	pomegranate juice	120 mL
¼ cup	dry red wine	60 mL
½ tsp.	salt	2.5 mL
½ tsp.	pepper	2.5 mL
2	racks of lamb or pork tenderloins, or 2 ½ lbs. (1.15 kg) flank steak	2

In a blender or food processor, purée all the ingredients except the meat. Pour the marinade over the meat. Cover and refrigerate for 6 hours or overnight. Before cooking, wipe off excess marinade.

Heat the grill or barbecue until quite hot, then (if you have this option) turn off one side of the grill and leave the other side on high. Place the meat on the side that's turned off and close the lid. The surface of the meat will sear while the inside cooks through without burning the outside.

When you're ready to flip the meat, turn off the hot side and turn on the other side. Flip the meat onto the side of the grill you have just turned off, close the lid and finish cooking to your taste.

This marinade does wonderful things for red meat. I first used it on lamb and many diners told me they had never liked lamb, but this was different: "It's good!" I knew the recipe was a keeper. I like to grill the marinated meat because the flavour is better with the searing you only get from a hot grill. Try using the marinade on kebabs for a rich flavour.

— Rosemary

Grilled Lamb in Asian Garlic & Red Wine Marinade

Lamb and rosemary have an affinity for each other. Cherished holidays on Saltspring Island with my friend dee and her family always saw one dinner of grilled Saltspring lamb that had been rubbed or marinated with rosemary. This recipe is not a holiday invention, but a definite favourite when it comes to simple summer fare. The marinade works well with most meats, if you aren't a fan of lamb. Serve with grilled spuds and a fresh garden salad.

— Janet

Serves 8 with leftovers

½ cup	soy sauce	120 mL
½ cup	olive oil	120 mL
½ cup	sesame oil	120 mL
½ cup	chopped parsley	120 mL
2	cloves garlic, finely chopped	2
1 Tbsp.	chopped fresh thyme	15 mL
2 Tbsp.	chopped fresh rosemary	30 mL
1 tsp.	dry mustard	5 mL
½ tsp.	mace	2.5 mL
½ tsp.	oregano	2.5 mL
2 cups	dry red wine (zinfandel, cabernet, merlot)	480 mL
1	leg of lamb, boned and tied	1

Combine all ingredients except the lamb in a bowl or pan large enough to hold the meat. Mix until the dry mustard is fully integrated. Remove 1 cup (240 mL) of the marinade and set aside. Place the lamb in the marinade, cover and refrigerate for 4 to 6 hours, turning every hour.

An hour before grilling, remove the lamb from the fridge and allow it to come to room temperature. Preheat the grill to high. Place the lamb on the grill and cook covered, turning every 15 minutes until it is medium-rare or your desired degree of doneness.

While the lamb is grilling, place the reserved marinade in a small sauté pan and reduce at medium-high until it thickens to sauce consistency, approximately 10 minutes. Allow the lamb to rest for 10 to 15 minutes before slicing and serving. Drizzle the sauce over the lamb and serve warm.

No-Salt Gravy

It's tough to fool someone who's been around since 1900, so when the doctor told my grandfather, Redvers Evans, to cut the salt out of his diet, some ingenious flavouring had to be done. Try adding lemon juice, wine or beer to your gravy in lieu of salt. The results are quite surprising!

— Rhondda Siebens

Olive-Marinated Leg of Lamb

Serves 6 to 8

1	4–5 lb. (2–2.25 kg) leg of lamb, boned and butterflied	1
2 cups	kalamata olives, pitted	480 mL
5	cloves garlic, peeled	5
5	anchovies, drained	5
½ cup	olive oil	120 mL
2 Tbsp.	capers	30 mL
2 Tbsp.	fresh sage leaves, chopped	30 mL
	zest of 1 orange	
	freshly ground black pepper to taste	

This dish is based on a recipe by Joyce Goldstein. The strong, earthy flavours in the marinade perfume the meat. Leftovers make delicious sandwiches (try a baguette, with mayo, red onion and mesclun greens), if you manage to save any!

— Pam

Place the lamb in a roasting pan with the outside of the leg down.

Place the remaining ingredients in a food processor and buzz to a paste. Spread the olive paste over the cut surfaces of the lamb, massaging into crevices. Cover and refrigerate overnight.

Preheat the oven to 400°F (200°C). Roast the lamb uncovered 1 ¼ to 1 ½ hours, until the internal temperature reaches 140°F (60°F) for medium-done meat. Let rest for 10 minutes before carving.

Soy Sauce

Soy sauce is the constant companion to Asian food preparation. It is a naturally fermented product of roasted soybeans and a grain, usually wheat, that is aged for up to two years. The first function of soy sauce is as a food preservative, but it also has the added bonus of being a highly nutritious and easily digested protein concentrate.

Dark soy is aged longer, and toward the end of the process molasses is added. It has a thicker consistency and caramel-like flavour. (Black soy sauce is an extra-concentrated type.) Light soy has a thin consistency and is saltier than the dark variety. Reach for the dark soy sauce when preparing heartier dishes, particularly with red meat, and use light soy sauce for more delicate preparations, including seafood and vegetables, and for dipping sauces.

Mushroom soy is flavoured with straw mushrooms. It is a full-flavoured sauce and should be used where a dark soy sauce is called for.

Tamari is a term often used, wrongly, to mean Japanese soy sauce. True tamari, rare even in Japan, is a rich, dark sauce made with no wheat.

— Gail Norton

Recommended beer or wine:
dark beer or New World
syrah or zinfandel

Lamb Curry

My taste buds have hovered for years above the intricacies of Indian curries, and I have finally settled—with a sigh of relief—into acceptance of Indian food as my all-time favourite. The richness, the complexity of flavours, the unending variants, the fabulous vegetable dishes . . . it always wows me. When you make this curry, make some naan (see Yeasted Flatbread, page 191) and cook a potful of basmati rice. Add a dish of Six-Fruit Chutney to the table, then sit down to a "fab" feast.

— dee

Serves 4 to 6

2 lbs.	lamb shoulder, cut into 2-inch (5-cm) cubes	1 kg
4	cloves garlic, minced	4
1 tsp.	freshly cracked black pepper	5 mL
2 Tbsp.	olive oil	30 mL
1	onion, cut into ½-inch (1.2-cm) dice	1
4	cloves garlic, minced	4
½ tsp.	ground fennel seed	2.5 mL
½ tsp.	ground cumin seed	2.5 mL
½ tsp.	ground fenugreek	2.5 mL
½ tsp.	ground coriander	2.5 mL
½ tsp.	turmeric	2.5 mL
1 tsp.	mustard seed	5 mL
1 tsp.	garam masala	5 mL
1 tsp.	Madras curry powder (see page 67)	5 mL
⅛ tsp.	ground cloves	.5 mL
½ tsp.	ground cinnamon	2.5 mL
½ tsp.	kalonji	2.5 mL
	hot chili flakes to taste	
¼ cup	tomato paste	60 mL
1 cup	water or stock	240 mL
1	19-oz. (532-mL) can chickpeas	1
	circle of parchment paper to fit inside cooking pan	
	salt and freshly ground black pepper to taste	
	lemon juice to taste	
	minced cilantro, for garnish	

Kalonji

Kalonji, although it is called black onion seed, is not from the onion family, but from the plant known to botanists as *Nigella*. It may also be mistakenly called black cumin seed, which, like kalonji, is native to northern India. Find it in East Indian spice markets.

— dee Hobsbawn-Smith

Combine the cubed lamb, 4 cloves garlic, pepper and 1 Tbsp. (15 mL) oil. Let stand while you prepare the spice blend. Preheat the oven to 325°F (165°C).

Heat a heavy-bottomed, ovenproof braising pan over medium-high heat, then add the remaining oil, the onion and 4 cloves garlic. Cook until the onion is tender and translucent, 5 to 7 minutes. Add all the spices, stir well and cook briefly, about 2 minutes, until the spices smell toasty. Add the tomato paste, water or stock, chickpeas and lamb mixture. Bring to a boil, then reduce heat to a simmer.

Cover the mixture with a piece of parchment paper that touches the surface of the meat, then cover snugly with aluminum foil and then the pan lid.

Place the pan in the oven and braise the lamb for 2 to 2 1/2 hours, until fork-tender. Skim off any extra fat, then season to taste with salt, pepper and lemon juice. Garnish with minced fresh cilantro just before serving.

Six-Fruit Chutney

Fresh fruit chutney requires very little effort once the initial peeling and chopping is completed. The time spent returns great dividends when the urge to eat an Indian curry overtakes the cook. Add a chutney, some naan and a potful of rice, and the table is transformed into a banquet fit to share with your very dearest companions. It's a kind of magic . . . from a few pieces of autumn fruit, a feast evolves.

Makes about 8 cups (2 L)

4	pears, peeled and cut into ½-inch (1.2-cm) dice	4
3	Granny Smith apples, peeled and cut into ½-inch (1.2-cm) dice	3
4	Gala apples, peeled and cut into ½-inch (1.2-cm) dice	4
1 cup	seedless Thompson raisins	240 mL
1 cup	frozen or fresh cranberries	240 mL
2 cups	brown sugar	480 mL
2 cups	apple cider or mint-infused vinegar	480 mL
2 Tbsp.	mustard seed	30 mL
1	orange, minced	1
1	grapefruit, minced	1

Combine all the ingredients in a heavy-bottomed pot. Bring to a boil, then reduce the heat and simmer 30 to 45 minutes, or until the chutney is thick and soft. Store in the fridge for up to 2 months.

pastas & grains

Quickie Pesto Sauce

My son plays soccer, and he insists that he eat two hours prior to games and practices. This pesto is really quick and stores forever in the fridge, which allows him to fix his own bowl of noodles without too much fuss and mess, which is good for any busy mom! He often adds cold cuts, roasted meats or vegetables, tomatoes or chopped-up greens.

— Janet

Makes three to four 6-oz. (180-mL) jars

2 cups	fresh basil leaves	480 mL
6 Tbsp.	toasted pine nuts (see page 171)	90 mL
4	cloves garlic, lightly crushed	4
pinch	salt	pinch
¾ cup	freshly grated Parmesan cheese	180 mL
½ cup	olive oil	120 mL
3 Tbsp.	unsalted butter, at room temperature	45 mL
	olive oil	

Put the basil, pine nuts, garlic and salt in a food processor. Pulse until blended into a paste. Add the cheese and combine. While the processor is running, drizzle the olive oil through the top. The pesto should be quite smooth and brilliant green. Quickly blend in the butter. Put the pesto into sterilized jars and top with a little olive oil. Refrigerate or freeze.

When adding the pesto to pasta, add 1 to 2 Tbsp. (15 to 30 mL) of the pasta water to improve the texture. Replace the olive oil on top of the pesto after each use. This helps preserve the pesto and that beautiful colour.

Cilantro Pesto

This is a refreshing variation on the classic basil pesto—and it enlivens any plain pasta. I also like to have pesto on hand to use in marinades and vinaigrettes or just to top a baked potato. Pesto freezes well if you leave out the cheese. I freeze it in small amounts in resealable plastic bags, then add the cheese after the pesto thaws.

— Ellen

Makes 1 ½ cups (360 mL)

3 cups	fresh cilantro leaves	720 mL
4–6	cloves garlic	4–6
½ cup	grated Parmesan cheese	120 mL
¼ cup	toasted walnuts (see page 171)	60 mL
	zest of 2 limes	
¼–½ cup	olive oil	60–120 mL
	salt and freshly ground black pepper to taste	

Combine the cilantro, garlic, cheese, walnuts and zest in a food processor. Pulse to chop coarsely. With the machine running slowly, add the olive oil. Season to taste with salt and pepper and process to your desired consistency. Let stand 5 to 10 minutes. Before tossing with hot pasta, add a little of the pasta water to help incorporate the pesto into the pasta.

Simple Tomato Sauce for Pasta

Makes enough for 4 to 6 servings

4–6 Tbsp.	olive oil	60–90 mL
8	cloves garlic, peeled and smashed	8
1	28-oz. (796-mL) can Italian plum tomatoes	1
2 tsp.	sea salt	10 mL
1	bunch fresh basil leaves	1
1/4 cup	freshly grated Parmesan	60 mL
1 Tbsp.	freshly cracked black pepper	15 mL

In a medium-size saucepan, heat the oil over medium heat. (Use enough oil to cover the bottom of the saucepan.) Add the garlic and cook, stirring, until fragrant, about 2 to 3 minutes. Be careful to not burn the garlic. Add the tomatoes and their juice, and the sea salt, and reduce the heat to low. Simmer 30 minutes, stirring occasionally.

Add the basil leaves only a few minutes before serving. Serve over cooked pasta (preferably spaghettini) with freshly grated Parmesan and freshly cracked black pepper.

Make this in the middle of the winter when real tomatoes on the vine are a lost species. I prefer it to chicken soup for its soul-warming properties.

— Karen

"How to Get Your Kids to Eat Mushrooms" Pasta Sauce

Most kids hate mushrooms! My son calls them poison: he won't even try a little taste! Ah, but being the evil mom that I am, and knowing how good they are for him, and wanting to try to keep the carnivores' meat consumption to a dull roar, I reinvented "meat sauce." He eats it, he loves it, and he has no idea what "poison" lurks in every mouthful. The key here is to make sure that the ground turkey or beef is prominently displayed during preparation, and the mushrooms are carefully hidden. (Hopefully my son will never read this cookbook!)

— Janet

Serves 6 to 8 ravenous soccer players

2 lbs.	ripe Roma tomatoes, tops trimmed	1 kg
2 cups	field mushrooms	480 mL
6 Tbsp.	olive oil	90 mL
1 cup	onions, chopped	240 mL
3	cloves garlic, minced	3
½ lb.	ground turkey or beef	225 g
1 cup	red wine	240 mL
1	bunch fresh basil leaves, chopped	1
	salt and freshly ground black pepper to taste	
	chili flakes to taste	
	white sugar to taste	
1 cup	grated Parmesan cheese, for garnish	240 mL

Preheat the oven to 375ºF (190ºC). Place the tomatoes and mushrooms in a single layer in a large roasting pan, drizzle lightly with 2 Tbsp. (30 mL) of the oil and roast uncovered for 1 hour, turning them every 15 minutes.

Meanwhile, heat the remaining oil in a large sauté pan on medium heat. Add the onions and sauté until soft and fragrant but not brown. Add the garlic and turkey or beef and cook until the meat is lightly browned, breaking it into bite-sized pieces as it cooks.

Once the tomatoes and mushrooms are done, add the tomatoes and any liquid to the onion-meat mixture. *Finely* chop the mushrooms to the texture of ground meat and add them to the onion-meat mixture. Turn up the heat to high, add the red wine and bring to a low boil. Reduce the heat to medium and allow the mixture to simmer for 15 to 20 minutes. Stir occasionally, breaking up the tomatoes into small pieces, or to the desired consistency.

Add the chopped basil, salt, pepper and chili flakes to taste. If the sauce is too astringent, add a small amount of white sugar to balance the flavours.

Serve over spaghetti or fettuccine and top with Parmesan.

Pasta with Lavender-Cream Vegetable Medley Sauce

Serves 4 to 6

1 Tbsp.	dried lavender flowers	15 mL
½ cup	apple cider vinegar	120 mL
⅓ cup	honey	80 mL
1	clove garlic, finely minced	1
1 tsp.	dried sage (optional)	5 mL
	salt to taste	
1 cup	whipping cream	240 mL
1 lb.	dried fusilli pasta	450 g
3 Tbsp.	olive oil	45 mL
1	large onion	1
2	cloves garlic, minced	2
2	sweet bell peppers (red, yellow or orange), cut into strips	2
1	small zucchini, cut into ¼-inch (.5-cm) rounds	1
6	baby carrots, each cut into 4 sticks	6
1	large fennel bulb, sliced	1
½ lb.	fresh salmon, cut into ½-inch (1-cm) cubes (optional)	225 g
	sliced green onions, for garnish	

Make sure you use culinary lavender that has not been sprayed with lavender-enhancing perfume or chemicals. Look for Okanagan Lavender Farm products; they are of excellent quality.

— Gail

In a saucepan on medium-low heat, combine the lavender, vinegar, honey, garlic and sage. Heat gently for about 30 minutes. Allow to cool, then strain. Add the salt and whipping cream to the lavender mixture, and simmer gently until it is quite thick, 20 to 30 minutes.

While the cream sauce is simmering, bring a large pot of salted water to a boil. Add the fusilli to the boiling water and cook until al dente, about 10 minutes. Drain pasta, toss with a bit of olive oil so it won't stick together if you are not using it immediately.

Meanwhile, heat a second pan over medium-high, add the olive oil and sauté the vegetables until al dente, about 5 minutes. Add the salmon pieces if desired, and continue to cook until the salmon is done, about 5 minutes more.

Toss together the vegetables and salmon, cream sauce and cooked pasta. Garnish with green onions.

Penne with Chèvre, Rapini & Caramelized Onions

*Quick, easy, delicious. . . . all the
prerequisites. Be sure to prepare
the Caramelized Onions before
cooking the pasta and rapini.
Serve with a salad of mixed
greens and good bread.*

— Ellen

Serves 4 to 6

1	bunch rapini, washed and chopped	1
2 Tbsp.	good-quality olive oil	30 mL
1	clove garlic, minced	1
	salt and freshly ground black pepper to taste	
1 lb.	dried penne	450 g
4–5 oz.	chèvre	115–140 g
1 recipe	Caramelized Onions	1 recipe

Bring a large pot of salted water to a boil. While waiting for the water to boil, prepare the rapini. Sauté the rapini in the olive oil over medium-high heat with the garlic, salt and pepper until wilted, 7 to 10 minutes. Set aside.

When the water is boiling, add the penne and cook until al dente, about 7 to 10 minutes. Drain, reserving a little of the pasta water. Toss the pasta with the chèvre, rapini and onions, using the pasta water to facilitate mixing.

Caramelized Onions

Serves 4 to 6

1 Tbsp.	butter	15 mL
1 Tbsp.	olive oil	15 mL
1	large, sweet onion, thinly sliced	1
2 Tbsp.	sherry	30 mL
	salt and freshly ground black pepper to taste	

Melt the butter and oil in a heavy-bottomed sauté pan, on medium heat. Cast iron is best, as it colours the onion quickly. Cook the onion, stirring and tossing frequently, until it starts to turn dark golden brown; this could take 15 to 20 minutes.

Pour in the sherry and scrape up the bits on the bottom. Season to taste with salt and pepper and keep warm.

Recommended wine: fleshy cabernet franc from southern France

Fusilli with Roasted Onions, Sun-Dried Tomatoes, Olives & Chèvre

Serves 4 to 6

2 lbs.	yellow onions	1 kg
2 tsp.	salt	10 mL
4 Tbsp.	olive oil	60 mL
2 tsp.	dried sage leaves	10 mL
1 tsp.	freshly ground black pepper	5 mL
2 Tbsp.	balsamic vinegar	30 mL
10	oil-packed sun-dried tomatoes, sliced	10
½ cup	oil-cured olives, sliced	120 mL
1 lb.	dried fusilli pasta	450 g
1 lb.	chèvre, crumbled into pieces	450 g
	finely chopped parsley, for garnish	

Preheat the oven to 375°F (190°C). Peel the onions and slice them into rounds about ½ inch (1.2 cm) thick. Separate the rings, then toss them with salt, olive oil, sage, pepper and balsamic vinegar.

Lightly oil a large baking dish with the oil from the sun-dried tomatoes, add the onions, cover with foil, and bake for 30 minutes. Remove the foil and stir, then cover again and bake for another 15 minutes until the onions are soft and beginning to brown.

Stir again, then add the sun-dried tomatoes and olives and return to the oven, uncovered, for 15 minutes or so until the juices are reduced to a syrup.

While the tomatoes and onions are baking, bring a large pot of salted water to a boil. Add the fusilli to the boiling water and cook until al dente, about 10 minutes. When the pasta is cooked, rinse and drain it, then toss the onion mixture with the pasta and chèvre. Garnish with parsley.

This luscious pasta dish has all of my favourite ingredients in one pot. The semi-caramelized onions tossed with the chèvre create a creamy, earthy sauce. You can leave out the sun-dried tomatoes if you wish, but the olives enliven the dish. The onions can be prepared ahead, then the remaining ingredients added to them when you are ready.

— Gail

Truffle Gnocchi with Fried Sage & Toasted Walnuts

To me, the key to great gnocchi is that they are tender; therefore, not too much flour and don't work the dough like bread dough or it will be tough. I learned to make perfect gnocchi while working under Julio Gonzales at Vancouver's famed Villa Del Lupo. I now understand what his perfectionism was all about. I taught my partner to make gnocchi and she now brags **her** recipe is the best! There are many variations on the basic method, so get a real feel for the dough and test it often as you add flour little by little. The best way to do that is to have a small pot of boiling water to poach a few as you work.

— Shelley

4 to 6 large servings		
4	large baker-style potatoes	4
1	egg	1
1 ½–2 lbs.	all-purpose flour	675–900 g
2	large fresh black truffles, finely chopped	2
2 Tbsp.	truffle oil	30 mL
	salt and freshly ground black pepper to taste	
½ cup	butter	120 mL
¼ cup	fresh sage leaves	60 mL
1 Tbsp.	Fleur de Sel	15 mL
½ cup	toasted walnuts, roughly chopped (see page 171)	120 mL

Boil the potatoes, skins on, completely immersed in water. Cook without a lid until the potatoes are tender when pierced with a fork and the skins are split. Drain the potatoes and allow them to air cool. When the potatoes are cool enough to handle, peel them and pass them through a food mill. If a food mill is not available, scrape the potatoes through a fine-mesh sieve.

Place the potatoes in a large mixing bowl or the bowl of a mixer with the paddle attachment. Beat by hand or run the machine on slow and add the egg, then begin adding some of the flour. The amount of moisture content in the potatoes will determine the amount of flour that you add, so each recipe may vary. A basic rule is 1 part potato to 1 ½ parts flour.

Add the truffles and oil and continue to add flour until the dough is well formed but not stiff. Add salt and pepper to taste. Test small amounts of dough by pulling off a thumb-size piece and poaching it until it surfaces. The texture should be firm but soft; if it is gummy at all it needs more flour.

Working on a floured surface with extra flour handy, begin cutting off strips of dough and rolling them out with both palms, pressing down and out in a back-and-forth motion. When the strips are the thickness of a wooden spoon handle, use a knife to cut off fingernail-size pieces of dough and place those in a pile of flour. Using your fingertip, press into the centre of each bit of dough and roll it toward you. Place it on a heavily floured tray.

When you have rolled out all the dough, you can freeze the gnocchi on trays and place in airtight containers for later use. They can be frozen for up to one month.

When you are ready to serve the gnocchi, bring a pot of salted water to a boil.

Melt the butter in a large sauté pan over medium heat. Add the sage leaves and continue to cook. The sage will start to crisp and the butter will become infused with the sage flavour.

Add the frozen or fresh gnocchi to the boiling water and remove them with a large slotted spoon as they float to the surface. Drain well and add to the sage butter. Toss the gnocchi in the butter to coat it and brown it a little.

Season with the Fleur de sel and divide the gnocchi among serving bowls. Drizzle some of the butter over top. Sprinkle with toasted walnuts and serve immediately.

Superior Salt: Fleur de Sel

Salt is salt, right? Wrong! Fleur de Sel is the Cadillac, the balsamic vinegar, virtually the reason for the existence of tomatoes. It is the most expensive salt in the world and when you consider how difficult it is to gather, it's no wonder. When the conditions are just right, when the sun is hot and the wind blows strongly, the salt blooms and crystallizes out of the saturated brine of salt marshes. It forms a fragile skin over the salty liquor.

For years, salt farmers broke up this top layer and mixed it into the layers of salt underneath. But French chefs discovered the superior flavour of the top layer the fleur de sel—and salt farmers were only too pleased to fill the new demand.

You can find it in specialty stores, especially those that carry French products. Use it as a condiment—sprinkled on food just before serving. Taste it next to your favourite salt and you'll notice the superior taste.

— Gail Norton

Dailyn's Squash & Wild Mushroom Ravioli with Chèvre Sauce

Kids love little packets of food. It seems to bring out the engineer or architect lurking in their future lives. Set a soup plate full of these lush bites in front of the junior cook who helped to fill them, and you may be amazed at the analytical dissection that takes place. Of course, older sibs might be tempted to count (very audibly) just how many ravioli constitute one bite—the ensuing competition might not be fit for the table! Fun comes in many forms.

— dee

Serves 8

2 lbs.	whole butternut or ambercup squash	1 kg
1 Tbsp.	grated fresh ginger root	15 mL
1 Tbsp.	unsalted butter	15 mL
1 Tbsp.	olive oil	15 mL
½ lb.	chanterelles	225 g
4	cloves garlic, minced	4
1 Tbsp.	minced fresh thyme	15 mL
	salt and freshly cracked black pepper to taste	
2	packages of square won ton wrappers	2
1	egg, well beaten, for sealing wrappers	1
2 cups	whipping cream	480 mL
½ lb.	chèvre, crumbled	225 g
3 Tbsp.	minced fresh thyme or lemon thyme	45 mL

Stab the squash several times with the tines of a fork, then bake it until tender in the oven. The actual temperature doesn't really matter; just stick the squash in whenever the oven is running anyway. The lower the temperature, the longer the squash will take to become tender. Let the squash cool, then split it open, scoop out and discard the seeds, and mash up the pulp in a large bowl. Add the ginger.

Heat the butter and oil over high heat in a large sauté pan and add the chanterelles. Cook them until tender, adding the garlic and 1 Tbsp. (15 mL) thyme as the mushrooms begin to soften. Season with salt and pepper to taste. Stir in the squash and ginger.

Open one package of won ton wrappers, remove a dozen or so, and cover the rest of the wrappers so they don't dry out. Lay a row of wrappers out on the counter and drop a small spoonful of filling onto each one.

Brush the edges with beaten egg, lay a second wrapper on top, matching the edges, and use the sides of your hands to push the top wrapper firmly onto the bottom wrapper and simultaneously squish out any air. Repeat with the remaining wrappers and filling. If your counter is cluttered with ravioli, dust baking sheets with cornstarch and arrange the ravioli on the dusted trays without overlapping edges or stacking. Wrap well and chill or freeze until you are ready to serve dinner.

To make the sauce, heat the cream to boiling, reduce until thickened, then stir in the chèvre without allowing the cream to return to the boil. Season with the 3 Tbsp. (45 mL) thyme, add salt and pepper to taste, and keep warm.

Put a large potful of salted water on to boil. When it reaches the boiling point, add as many fresh or frozen ravioli as the pot can comfortably accommodate. Be prepared to work in batches unless you have a very big pot. Cook the ravioli for about 5 minutes, or until the won ton wrappers are translucent and tender. Drain gently through a colander, divide evenly among heated soup plates, and drizzle the sauce over top. Serve hot.

Chicken & Leek Cannelloni with Apple Balsamic Sauce

The idea of make-ahead recipes is not exclusive to busy home cooks. Restaurants also depend on certain menu items that are made in batches and frozen until ready to use. By no means does this diminish the quality of the finished dish. For a home chef, a few good recipes made ahead and frozen mean that you can entertain on a moment's notice and stay relaxed.

— Shelley

Serves 8

4	large chicken breasts, boneless and skinless	4
3	medium-sized leeks, cut diagonally in ¼-inch (.6-cm) slices	3
2 Tbsp.	butter	30 mL
1 recipe	Béchamel Sauce	1 recipe
2 cups	mascarpone cheese	480 mL
½ cup	Parmesan cheese	120 mL
1 Tbsp.	lemon zest	15 mL
1 Tbsp.	lemon juice	15 mL
½ tsp.	freshly ground nutmeg	2.5 mL
	salt and freshly ground black pepper to taste	
16	5- x 5-inch (12.5- x 12.5-cm) fresh pasta sheets	16
2 cups	half-and-half cream	480 mL
1 recipe	Apple Balsamic Sauce	1 recipe

Preheat the oven to 375ºF (190ºC). Place the chicken breasts on a baking sheet and season with salt and pepper. Bake for 15 to 20 minutes or until cooked through. Do not overcook the chicken or the mixture will be very dry. Cool the chicken. If you have a grinder, coarse-grind the chicken; otherwise, use a food processor on "pulse" mode to achieve a pulpy texture. Scrape the chicken into a large bowl.

Sauté the sliced leeks in butter until soft and translucent, then add to the ground chicken. Stir in the Béchamel Sauce, mascarpone, Parmesan, lemon zest and juice, and nutmeg. Season with salt and pepper to taste.

Bring a large pot of salted water to a boil. Add the pasta sheets to the pot several at a time. Remove the sheets after 1 minute and plunge them into a bowl of ice water to cool. As the sheets are cooked and cooled, lay them out on clean linen kitchen towels and cover with more clean towels until ready to begin assembling the cannelloni.

Put some of the chicken mixture into a pastry bag without a tip. Pipe the mixture onto one edge of the sheet. Roll each sheet up around the filling and place onto a plastic wrap–lined baking sheet. Be sure the cannelloni are not touching each other or they will stick together if frozen.

At this point, the cannelloni can be refrigerated for up to 2 days or frozen for up to 1 week. (Defrost in the fridge overnight before baking.)

Preheat the oven to 375ºF (190ºC). Place the cannelloni in a baking dish and add the cream and half of the Apple Balsamic Sauce. Cover and bake for 15 to 20 minutes, until heated through.

Remove from the baking dish and arrange on serving plates. Garnish with the remaining warm apple sauce.

Béchamel Sauce

Makes about 2 ½ cups (600 mL)

⅓ cup	butter	80 mL
1	small onion, finely diced	1
⅓ cup	flour	80 mL
2 cups	2% or whole milk	480 mL
½ tsp.	freshly ground nutmeg	2.5 mL
	salt and freshly ground black pepper to taste	

Melt the butter over low heat in a small pot and add the onion. Stir in the flour and cook, stirring constantly, until the flour turns light brown. Slowly whisk in the milk and continue to stir until the mixture has thickened, about 10 to 15 minutes.

Season with nutmeg, salt and pepper. Pour into a bowl, cover with plastic wrap and set aside to cool.

Apple Balsamic Sauce

Makes 2 cups (480 mL)

2 Tbsp.	sugar	30 mL
4	Golden Delicious apples, peeled, cored and chopped	4
4 Tbsp.	butter	60 mL
1 cup	chicken stock	240 mL
½ cup	balsamic vinegar	120 mL
¼ tsp.	ground cloves	1.2 mL

Place the sugar in a large sauté pan. Stir over high heat until the sugar is liquid and caramelized to a dark brown. Add the apples, tossing to prevent burning. Add ½ the butter, and all of the chicken stock and balsamic vinegar. Cook on medium-high until the liquid is reduced by half and the apples are soft. Season with cloves.

Remove from the heat and purée until smooth. Before serving, heat over medium heat and stir in the remaining butter.

Fettuccine with Sausage, Asparagus & Lemon Cream

This pasta dish is quick, easy and wonderful. It also lends itself to your versatility, taste or whatever is in your fridge at the time. Feel free to use different pasta, vegetables (peas, green beans, broccoli) or meats (chicken, ham, shrimp—or none).

— Rosemary

Serves 4 to 6

1 lb.	mild or spicy Italian sausage	450 g
½ lb.	asparagus	225 g
1 lb.	dried fettucine	450 g
½ cup	whipping cream	120 mL
½ cup	yogurt	120 mL
1 Tbsp.	lemon zest	15 mL
½ cup	Parmesan cheese, grated	120 mL
	salt and freshly ground black pepper to taste	
1 Tbsp.	chopped fresh chives	15 mL

Sauté or grill the sausage just until done, about 10 minutes depending on thickness. When cool, cut into bite-size pieces. Set aside.

Blanch the asparagus in boiling water for 2 minutes. Drain and rinse in cold water. Cut into bite-size pieces.

Bring a large pot of salted water to a boil. Add the pasta and cook at a rolling boil for 8 to 10 minutes. It should be al dente.

While the pasta is cooking, in a large saucepan combine the cream, yogurt and lemon zest. Add the asparagus and cook for 2 minutes over medium heat.

Drain the pasta. Add the pasta and sausage to the lemon cream. Gently stir in the cheese and add salt and pepper to taste. Garnish with chives before serving.

Dried Pastas

There is nothing quite so disappointing as a pasta dish where the sauce sinks to the bottom and the pasta sits on top. This can be prevented, in part, by buying a superior dried pasta.

It begins with good ingredients, like semolina, and a slightly roughened surface. Specialty dried pasta is made using bronze cast dies, unlike more commercial pasta made using Teflon-coated dies. The bronze dies rough up the surface as the pasta is extruded, which gives your sauce a surface to cling to.

But as Peter Bellusi of Calgary's Italian Gourmet Foods said, trust your taste. Some of the "rough surfaces" are only marketing strategies. Just because a pasta has a rough surface, that doesn't make it a superior pasta—surface should never replace quality ingredients.

— Gail Norton

Recommended beer or wine:
Thai beer or French columbard/
trebbiano blanc blend

Judy's Asian Noodles

Serves 6

½ lb.	rice noodles	225 g
½ lb.	beef, sliced into thin strips	225 g
3	cloves garlic, peeled and finely chopped	3
1 Tbsp.	ginger, peeled and finely chopped	15 mL
2 Tbsp.	oil	30 mL
1	red pepper, thinly sliced	1
½	yellow pepper, thinly sliced	¹/₂
2	carrots, peeled and thinly sliced	2
¼ lb.	snowpeas, with stems and fibre removed	115 g
2	green onions, sliced	2
2 Tbsp.	fresh cilantro, coarsely chopped	30 mL
1 recipe	Thai Sauce	1 recipe

Place the noodles in a bowl, cover with cold water and set aside. Combine the beef with the garlic and ginger, mixing thoroughly, and set aside.

Bring 4 quarts (1 L) of water to a boil. Remove the noodles from the cold water, then drop them into the boiling water for about 2 minutes. Drain and set aside.

Heat the oil in a large frying pan or wok over medium-high. Add the beef and stir-fry for 3 minutes. Add the peppers and carrots and stir-fry for 3 minutes. Add the snowpeas, green onion and cilantro and stir-fry for 2 minutes. Stir in the Thai Sauce, bring to a boil and serve.

Thai Sauce

Makes 1 ½ cups (360 mL)

2 Tbsp.	cornstarch	30 mL
⅓ cup	chicken stock	80 mL
¼ cup	sherry	60 mL
¼ cup	dark soy sauce	60 mL
¼ cup	corn syrup	60 mL
2 Tbsp.	oyster sauce	30 mL
2 Tbsp.	chili sauce	30 mL
2 tsp.	sesame seed oil	10 mL

Mix the cornstarch with 2 Tbsp. cold water and set aside. Place the remaining ingredients in a saucepan and bring to a boil. Quickly whisk in the cornstarch and boil the sauce for 5 minutes, whisking frequently.

It's the rich sauce and rice noodles that make this dish! You can create many variations, depending on your likes and dislikes. The sauce can be kept in the fridge for at least a week.

— Judy

Recommended wine: white
burgundy, preferably Chablis

Lobster Perogies in Sweet Tomato Basil Cream

My grandmother "Stevie," as her
friends called her, taught me the
importance of group effort. In
other words, many hands get the
job done quicker! Enlist your
friends, kids, roommates and part-
ners and make a large batch of
these. Freeze on baking sheets
lined with parchment paper
overnight, then store in plastic
containers. Take out only what
you need when you need it.
They don't need to be thawed
before cooking.

— Shelley

Serves 20 (5 perogies per serving)

1 ½ lbs.	cooked lobster meat, chopped into medium-size chunks	680 g
3 cups	cold mashed potatoes (leftovers are great!)	720 mL
1 cup	Crème Fraîche (page 212)	240 mL
¼ cup	fresh chopped tarragon, stems trimmed off	60 mL
½ cup	lobster bisque (canned is okay)	120 mL
	kosher salt and freshly ground white pepper to taste	
1	package oriental dumpling wrappers (approximately 100 wrappers per package)	1
1 recipe	Sweet Tomato Basil Cream	1 recipe

In a medium-sized bowl, combine the lobster meat,
potatoes, Crème Fraîche, tarragon and lobster bisque.
Season to taste with salt and pepper.

Place several wrappers on a clean work surface. Put
1 Tbsp. (15 mL) of filling on each wrapper just off the
centre. Brush each wrapper lightly with water, fold the
top over the filling and use your fingertips to seal the
edges.

Place the filled perogies on a baking sheet lined with
parchment paper, but do not overlap them or they will
stick together. Continue until all the filling has been
used. At this point, the perogies can be refrigerated
for up to 2 hours or frozen for 1 to 2 weeks.

To cook, bring a large pot of salted water to a boil.
Cook about 20 at a time, boiling until they "float to the
top." Remove and finish in the Sweet Tomato Basil
Cream sauce or serve the sauce under or over
the perogies.

Sweet Tomato Basil Cream

Makes 16 cups (4 L)

3 Tbsp.	olive oil	45 mL
1	small onion, chopped fine	1
6	cloves garlic, minced	6
2	shallots, minced	2
1 Tbsp.	chili flakes (optional)	15 mL
3	anchovy fillets, chopped to a paste	3
2 Tbsp.	dry oregano	30 mL
⅓ cup	tomato paste	80 mL
1	100-oz. (3-L) can of Italian plum tomatoes (It is important to use only the best.)	1
	kosher salt and freshly ground black pepper to taste	
½ lb.	fresh basil, thinly sliced	225 g
1 cup	whipping cream	240 mL
2 Tbsp.	cold butter	30 mL

In a heavy-bottomed pot over medium-high heat, heat the olive oil. Add the onion, garlic, shallot and chili, if using. Stir constantly until the garlic begins to take on colour. Add the anchovies, oregano and tomato paste and reduce the heat to medium.

Place a strainer or colander over the cooking pot and pour in the tomatoes, allowing the juice to run through and reserving the tomatoes. Squeeze the tomatoes with your hand to crush them, then pour the crushed tomatoes in with the rest of the mixture. Reduce the heat to low and continue to stir occasionally for about 1 hour. Season to taste with salt and pepper.

Stir in the basil, whipping cream and butter just before serving.

Chicken Risotto with Vanilla

Vanilla and asparagus are a heavenly match. The addition of vanilla creates an intriguing flavour.

— Gail

Serves 4 to 6

1 oz.	dried mushrooms	30 g
1 cup	wine, sherry or water	240 mL
1 Tbsp.	butter	15 mL
1 Tbsp.	olive oil	15 mL
3	1-inch (2.5-cm) pieces vanilla bean, cut lengthwise and seeds scraped out	3
1	small onion, chopped	1
2	cloves garlic, minced	2
½ cup	sliced button mushrooms	120 mL
1 cup	arborio rice	240 mL
¾ cup	white wine	180 mL
3 cups	chicken stock, heated	720 mL
1	boneless chicken breast, cooked and cut into ½-inch (1.25-cm) cubes	1
¾ cup	chopped asparagus	180 mL

Rehydrate the dried mushrooms in the wine, sherry or water for up to 4 hours.

Melt the butter and olive oil over medium heat, add the vanilla bean and heat briefly. Add the onion and garlic, and cook until soft, about 10 minutes. Add the rehydrated dried mushrooms (save the rehydrating liquid) and fresh mushrooms and sauté for about 3 minutes.

Add the rice, then the white wine, and reduce until there is no liquid remaining in the pan. Add the liquid from the mushrooms, then add the stock, ½ cup (125 mL) at a time, stirring constantly. Make sure all the stock has been absorbed before adding more.

When all the stock has been added and the rice is soft (about 25 minutes), add the chicken and asparagus. Heat through. Serve immediately.

Rehydrating Mushrooms

To rehydrate mushrooms, soak them in wine, sherry, stock or just water. If you have time to give them a longer soak—about 4 hours—the flavour is greatly enhanced. Make sure to save the soaking liquid to use in your dish. If you are time-challenged, pour boiling liquid over the mushrooms to speed the time up.

— Gail Norton

Squash & Arugula Risotto

Serves 4 to 6

1 ½ cups	puréed butternut squash	360 mL
1 Tbsp.	each olive oil and butter	15 mL
2 cups	coarsely chopped arugula	480 mL
4 Tbsp.	olive oil	60 mL
½ cup	finely chopped shallots	120 mL
2 cups	arborio rice	480 mL
½ cup	white wine	120 mL
6 cups	warm vegetable or chicken stock	1.5 L
½ cup	freshly grated Parmesan cheese	120 mL
3 Tbsp.	butter	45 mL
	salt and freshly ground black pepper to taste	

Preheat the oven to 375ºF (190ºC). Bake the butternut squash for 45 to 60 minutes until easily pierced with a skewer. Cool, peel and mash.

Sauté the arugula in the first amount of olive oil and butter over medium heat until wilted. Set aside.

In the same pan, sauté the shallots in the 4 Tbsp. (60 mL) olive oil until soft. Add the rice and continue to cook, stirring, until the rice begins to become translucent. Add the wine and cook until it is absorbed, still stirring.

Start adding warm stock by the ladleful, stirring between additions. As the stock is absorbed, add another ladleful. Continue in this manner until almost all the stock is incorporated. Add the squash with the last bit of stock. The rice should be just slightly firm, but tender and creamy. The cooking time after the first liquid has been added should be about 25 minutes.

Remove from the heat and stir in the cheese, butter and arugula. Season with salt and pepper. Serve immediately, as risotto does not hold well.

Don't be afraid of making risotto; just take your time and give it the full 25 to 30 minutes. Swiss chard or even spinach could be substituted for the arugula.

— Ellen

Prawn Basil Barley Risotto

*Although risotto is a labour-
intensive job, the resultant
creamy rich texture and
flavours of this dish make
it all worthwhile.*

— Judy

Serves 4

2 ½ cups	chicken or fish stock	600 mL
2 Tbsp.	butter	30 mL
1	shallot, peeled and finely chopped	1
1	clove garlic, minced	1
¼ lb.	arborio rice	115 g
¼ lb.	pearl barley	115 g
¼ cup	whipping cream	60 mL
3 Tbsp.	Parmesan cheese	45 mL
2 Tbsp.	fresh basil, coarsely chopped	30 mL
32	prawns, peeled	32
	salt and freshly ground black pepper to taste	

Place the stock into a pot, bring to a boil and set aside. In another pot, heat the butter, shallots and garlic over low for 2 minutes. Add the rice and barley and stir well. Gradually add the stock, ¹/₂ cup (120 mL) at a time, stirring constantly. Add more stock only when the previous addition has been absorbed.

Once all the stock has been incorporated, add the cream, Parmesan, basil and prawns, stirring constantly for about 3 minutes, until the prawns are bright pink. Season with salt and pepper and serve immediately.

Risotto Rice: Arborio, Vialone Nano, Carnaroli

There are several different risotto rices and each provides a different finished dish. The three that are readily available and of exceptional quality are arborio, vialone nano and carnaroli.

Arborio is a large, plump grain and produces a stickier risotto due to its higher soft starch content. It is great for compact styles of risotto, popular in Lombardy.

Vialone nano is a stubby, small grain that has a high starch content, but a tough kind of starch that doesn't soften easily in cooking. It is popular in Venice where the risotto's consistency is looser. The rice has a distinct resistance to the bite.

Carnaroli was developed by a Milanese rice grower who crossed vialone nano with a Japanese strain. Carnaroli is more expensive than the others, but Marcella Hazan, doyen of Italian cooking, feels that it is the most excellent of the three. The kernel has a soft starch that dissolves, but it also contains a tougher starch than the other varieties so that it cooks to a nice firm consistency.

—Gail Norton

Barley Pilaf Topped with an Olive Tapenade

Serves 4 to 6

2 Tbsp.	olive oil	30 mL
1	medium onion, minced	1
2	cloves garlic, minced	2
½ cup	minced fresh herbs (basil, thyme, parsley, sage)	120 mL
1 cup	barley	240 mL
3 cups	chicken broth	720 mL
	salt and freshly ground black pepper to taste	
½ cup	sliced green olives or bottled olive tapenade	120 mL
	chopped parsley, for garnish	

Heat a sauté pan over medium heat, add the olive oil and cook the onion and garlic until soft and cooked through, about 10 minutes. Stir in the mixed herbs and barley, tossing well to coat. Add the stock and heat to boiling.

Reduce the heat and simmer, covered, until all the liquid has been absorbed and the barley is tender, 35 to 40 minutes. If the barley seems too chewy, add more broth and continue to cook until done. Add salt and pepper to taste.

To serve, garnish portions with a generous dollop of chopped olives or tapenade and parsley.

Barley has usually been relegated to the bottom of the soup bowl, but with this recipe it shines all by itself. I use barley anywhere that calls for wild rice or brown rice—since the cooking time is roughly the same it is an easy switch. The barley always has a wonderful chewy texture with nutty aftertaste.

— Gail

Spicy Sesame Millet Pilaf with Roasted Red Peppers

Millet is a delicious grain that is most familiar to people as bird food. We are now realizing why the birds are so wacky about the grain. It has one of the highest protein content of any grain and a wonderful nutty flavour.

— Gail

Serves 4 to 6

¾ cup	millet	180 mL
3 Tbsp.	olive oil	45 mL
1	onion, chopped	1
2	cloves garlic, minced	2
1	red pepper, chopped	1
2 cups	chicken stock	480 mL
1	red pepper, roasted, peeled and chopped (see page 54)	1
1 Tbsp.	chili oil	15 mL
1 Tbsp.	red wine vinegar	15 mL
1 tsp.	sesame oil	5 mL
	salt and freshly ground black pepper to taste	
	minced parsley, for garnish	

Put the millet in a dry pan over medium heat and toast until it is brown and starts to pop, about 4 to 5 minutes.

Remove the millet from the pan, then add the olive oil and sauté the onion, garlic, and unroasted red peppers until soft and fragrant, about 10 to 15 minutes. Stir in the toasted millet and stock. Heat to boiling, then reduce the heat to simmer until the millet is tender and all the liquid is gone, about 20 minutes.

Stir in the roasted red pepper, chili oil, red wine vinegar and sesame oil and fluff with a fork. Season to taste with salt and pepper and garnish with minced parsley.

Millet

More commonly known as birdseed, this grain's most amazing characteristic is that it swells to five times its original size . . . a handful goes a long way. Millet has a wonderful nutty flavour and a handful adds a nice textural element to breads. It also has a very high protein content and a higher oil content, so store it in a cool, dark place. (I usually keep the container in the fridge.)

It is one of the hardiest grains and grows in arid climates where all else fails. The husk is quite hard and takes a while to soften. Toasting the seed before cooking helps to reduce the cooking time.

— Gail Norton

Israeli Couscous with Roasted Corn & Saffron

Serves 8

2 cups	corn kernels, fresh or frozen	480 mL
1	sweet red pepper, diced	1
1 Tbsp.	olive oil	15 mL
2 cups	Israeli couscous	480 mL
4 cups	chicken or vegetable stock	1 L
pinch	saffron	pinch
2	limes, juice and zest	2
2 Tbsp.	honey	30 mL
4 Tbsp.	extra virgin olive oil	60 mL
	sea salt and freshly ground black pepper to taste	
1	bunch fresh cilantro leaves	1

Israeli couscous is a larger version of the more commonly sold couscous. It looks like pasta and is very easy to make. It can be baked in the oven or cooked on top of the stove and, like regular couscous, is good served hot or at room temperature.

— Karen

Preheat the oven to 400°F (200°C). Place the corn kernels and diced red pepper in a baking pan and toss with the olive oil. Roast, stirring often, until the vegetables start to turn brown, about 10 to 15 minutes.

Meanwhile, in a medium saucepan, add the couscous to the stock and bring to a boil. Add the saffron and reduce heat to low. Simmer, covered, until the couscous is cooked through, about 20 minutes. Remove from the heat and stir with a fork to separate the grains. Add the roasted corn and red peppers.

Make a dressing by whisking together the lime juice, lime zest, honey and olive oil. Add salt and pepper to taste, then pour the dressing over the couscous and toss carefully. Taste again once all the ingredients are mixed, and adjust if necessary.

Garnish with fresh cilantro leaves and serve hot or at room temperature.

Cinnamon-Scented Couscous

*Couscous and cinnamon are
one of those food matches made
in heaven. This easy but
richly flavoured recipe makes a
superb side dish with roast
chicken or pork.*

— Gail

Serves 4 to 6

1 ¼ cups	chicken stock	300 mL
1 Tbsp.	ground cinnamon	15 mL
1 Tbsp.	olive oil	15 mL
8	fresh shiitake or domestic mushrooms, sliced	8
3	cloves garlic, minced	3
2 tsp.	cumin powder	10 mL
	salt and freshly ground black pepper to taste	
1	bunch green onions, sliced	1
1 cup	couscous	240 mL

In a small pot over medium-high heat, bring the chicken stock and cinnamon to a boil.

Heat a sauté pan over medium-high, add the olive oil and sauté the mushrooms, garlic, cumin, salt and pepper until the mushrooms are soft and cooked through, about 10 minutes. Add the green onions and cook until slightly soft, about 4 minutes.

Stir the couscous into the mushroom mixture and toss to coat the grains. Add the boiling stock, remove from the heat, cover and let stand for about 10 minutes. Fluff up the grains with a fork and serve.

Couscous

Couscous was my first revelatory grain experience. It is a semolina product that has been processed and dusted with flour. The only couscous available locally is the quick-cooking variety, so within 15 minutes you have a finished dish. Cook all your other ingredients before adding the couscous because it cooks so quickly.

Some books use a 2-to-1 ratio of liquid to the couscous, but I find the resulting consistency too gummy. Try the 1-to-1 ratio and add more liquid if you prefer a softer grain.

After adding the boiling liquid to the couscous, it's important not to continue heating the dish. The couscous becomes overcooked if left on heat.

— Gail Norton

vegetables & legumes

Grilled Marinated Endive

I love the bitterness of endive but some people find it a difficult taste sensation, so I marinate the endive in a bit of maple syrup and balsamic vinegar to temper the bitterness and add an extra flavour dimension. Don't marinate the endive for too long or they will become sodden and you'll lose the freshness of the vegetable.

— Gail

Serves 6 to 8

½ cup	balsamic vinegar	120 mL
¼ cup	maple syrup	60 mL
	salt and freshly ground black pepper to taste	
15	heads purple Belgian endive	15
2 Tbsp.	olive oil (optional)	30 mL

Combine the vinegar, maple syrup, salt and pepper to make a marinade. Cut the endives in half lengthwise and pour the marinade over top. Marinate in the refrigerator or at room temperature for at least 1 hour, and 3 hours at the most.

Heat the grill and cook the endives over medium heat until slightly brown and soft, about 5 minutes. Transfer to a serving dish and drizzle with olive oil, if desired.

Prosciutto-Wrapped Endive

This simple dish is exquisitely rich. The bitterness of the endive is cut with the creaminess of the cheese and the prosciutto adds a touch of nuttiness. Tallegio cheese is like a big-flavour Italian Brie. You can also try any creamy, full-flavoured soft cheese.

— Gail

Serves 8 to 10

15	heads Belgian endive	15
15	thin slices prosciutto	15
1 cup	whipping cream	240 mL
1 cup	rich chicken stock	240 mL
4 oz.	Tallegio cheese, grated	115 g

Preheat the oven to 375ºF (190ºC). Wrap the heads of endive with prosciutto and lay them in a 9- x 13-inch (23- x 33-cm) casserole pan. They should all fit together snugly in a single layer. Add the cream and enough chicken stock to cover the endive.

Bake uncovered in the oven until the endive is very soft, about 1 hour. Add more stock or cream as needed so that the pan does not become dry before the endive is soft. Sprinkle the cheese on top and bake until bubbly and slightly brown, about 5 to 10 minutes. Serve hot.

Blood Orange Braised Fennel

Serves 4

2 Tbsp.	good-quality olive oil	30 mL
1	clove garlic, sliced	1
4	medium fennel bulbs, trimmed and cut into 6 wedges, stems intact	4
	salt and freshly ground black pepper to taste	
½ cup	chicken or vegetable stock	120 mL
2	blood oranges, juice and zest	2

Heat the oil over medium heat in a heavy sauté pan and add the garlic. Add the fennel and season with salt and pepper. Turn the fennel wedges often to caramelize all sides, 10 to 15 minutes. Remove the garlic if it starts to turn brown. Add the stock, orange juice and zest (and a splash of wine if you happen to have some on hand). Cover and cook slowly until tender, about 20 minutes.

Braised fennel is one of the most succulent things in the world. Enough said.

— Ellen

Marinated Eggplant

Serves 4 to 6

4	Japanese eggplants (or 2 globe eggplants)	4
	salt	
	olive oil	
2	medium Roma tomatoes, cut into ½-inch (1-cm) dice	2
¾ cup	finely chopped green onion	180 mL
¼ cup	chopped parsley	60 mL
¼ cup	chopped cilantro	60 mL
¼ cup	red wine vinegar	60 mL
1 tsp.	ground cumin seeds	5 mL
dash	hot chili sauce	dash
	salt to taste	

Delicious on its own, this recipe is also great turned into a pasta dish. Just toss the eggplant with your favourite cooked pasta.

— Gail

Slice the eggplant into rounds ¼ inch (.6 cm) thick. Place them in a colander set over a bowl and sprinkle with salt. Allow the eggplant to drain for 30 minutes.

Preheat the oven to 400°F (200°C). Brush a cookie sheet with olive oil and place the eggplant in the oil, flipping the rounds so both sides are oiled. Bake until one side is slightly crispy and brown, about 10 minutes, then flip and brown the other side. Cut into strips.

Combine the remaining ingredients. Add the eggplant and stir. Cover and let stand for several hours. Serve at room temperature.

Grilled Portobello & Yam Terrine with Bleu de Causse

Bleu de Causse is a cheese from approximately the same region as Roquefort. It is unbelievably creamy and quite mild for a blue. I love it and it makes a perfect foil for the rich earthy flavours of the other ingredients. Do not serve this terrine cold—it is much better at room temperature. Serve it on its own or with simply dressed salad greens.

— Shelley

Serves 8

3	large yams or sweet potatoes	3
5	large Portobello mushroom caps	5
¼ cup	olive oil	60 mL
2 Tbsp.	balsamic vinegar	30 mL
1	clove garlic, finely minced	1
2 Tbsp.	fresh thyme, finely chopped	30 mL
	salt and freshly ground black pepper to taste	
2 Tbsp.	olive oil	30 mL
2 tsp.	lemon zest, finely chopped	10 mL
½ lb.	Bleu de Causse cheese	225 g
½ cup	Chive Oil (see page 58)	120 mL
16	fresh chive sprigs	16

Peel the yams and trim off both ends. Using a very sharp knife, trim the sides to make the yam into a rectangle shape. Using a mandolin, slice the yam into ⅛-inch (.35-cm) slices lengthwise. Bring a large pot of salted water to a boil and blanch the yam slices for 20 to 30 seconds. Remove and immediately place on a cooling rack.

Preheat a barbecue or grill to medium. Remove the stems and gills from the mushroom caps. Mix together the ¼ cup (60 mL) olive oil, vinegar, garlic and fresh thyme. Brush the mushroom caps generously with the oil mixture and set aside for 10 to 15 minutes. Reapply the oil mixture to the mushroom caps every 10 minutes until it has all been absorbed. Season the caps with salt and pepper and grill each side for at least 5 minutes. Remove the caps and cool completely.

Brush the yam slices with 2 Tbsp. (30 mL) olive oil and season well with salt. Grill both sides just enough to achieve grill marks, then sprinkle with lemon zest and let cool.

Place the cheese into a mixing bowl or the bowl of a food processor and blend the cheese until it has a smooth consistency. Do not overwork the cheese or it will melt.

Brush the inside of a loaf pan with a little oil, place plastic wrap on the inside of the pan so that it overhangs by 4 inches (10 cm). Press the wrap well into the corners and sides. Trim the yam slices to fit into the bottom of the loaf pan. Try not to overlap the slices too much; take the time to get the slices to fit together in a single layer.

Spread a thin layer of cheese over the yams. Slice the mushroom caps into several layers (depending on their thickness) crosswise. As with the yams, trim the mushroom pieces to fit on top of the yam and cheese in a single layer. Spread a thin layer of cheese over the mushroom slices.

Continue layering yam, cheese, mushroom, cheese, yam, cheese, etc. until you finish with a layer of yam. Pull the overhanging plastic up and over the top of the terrine to enclose it. Place heavy cans or a brick on top of the terrine to press it into the loaf pan.

Refrigerate 8 hours before removing the weight and unmolding the terrine. Use a very sharp and thin knife to slice portions. Place the slices on plates and drizzle with Chive Oil. Lay 2 chive sprigs on top of each terrine slice.

Recommended wine:
Alsatian riesling or pinot blanc,
or Italian pinot grigio

Steamed Fingerling Potatoes with Pancetta & Truffle Beurre Blanc

As I am an extremely inattentive gardener, with two wild dogs sure to trample any planting project, I planted a small potato patch in the southern-exposed back lane. To my shock and delight, the patch yielded about 10 pounds of long, nubby, fingerlike yellow beauties. As a proud first-timer, I gave away a third of my coveted first crop and ate the rest.

The following recipe reveals the embellishments used to complement the fruit of my labour. I now rely on the skill of the many local farmers to supply the additional 200 pounds (100 Kilograms) needed to create this dish each season.

— Shelley

Serves 4 side portions or 1 hungry gardener

2 lbs.	fingerling or yellow-fleshed baby potatoes, as fresh as possible	1 kg
4	slices pancetta, thinly sliced	4
4 oz.	Tallegio cheese (use a good Brie if Tallegio is not available)	115 g
1 recipe	Truffle Beurre Blanc	1 recipe
¼ cup	fresh chives, finely diced, for garnish	60 mL

Scrub the potatoes well but do not peel. Boil in plenty of salted water until they are just tender, about 10 to 15 minutes. Cool under cold running water, slice in half lengthwise and set aside until ready to serve.

Preheat the oven to 400°F (200°C). Place the pancetta on a baking sheet and put into the oven for 3 to 5 minutes, or until the pancetta is crisp and lightly golden. Place on a kitchen towel to drain.

To serve, place a steamer basket over a pot of simmering water. Place the sliced potatoes in a single layer on the bottom of the steamer basket. (It may be necessary to do several batches, depending on the size of the steamer.) Cover the basket with a lid and allow the potatoes to steam for 2 to 3 minutes.

Cut the Tallegio into thin slices. Carefully remove the lid and add the cheese slices on top of the potatoes, then cover again for 2 minutes or just until the cheese begins to melt. Remove the basket from the simmering water.

Divide the potatoes among serving plates, placing them in the centre. Crumble a pancetta slice over each potato pile, drizzle some of the Truffle Beurre Blanc on and around the potatoes, and finish with a generous sprinkling of fresh chives.

Truffle Beurre Blanc

Makes 1 cup (240 mL)

1 tsp.	truffle oil	5 mL
1	shallot, peeled and diced	1
1	bay leaf	1
1 tsp.	white peppercorns	5 mL
¼ cup	white wine vinegar	60 mL
½ cup	white wine	120 mL
1	black truffle, very thinly sliced	1
½ lb.	unsalted butter, cold and cut into small cubes	225 g
	salt to taste	

In a small saucepan over medium heat, warm the truffle oil. Add the shallot, bay leaf and peppercorns and stir to coat. Add the vinegar, wine and half of the black truffle slices. Simmer until the liquid is reduced by two-thirds.

Remove from the heat and carefully take out the peppercorns and bay leaf with a spoon. Return the pot to low heat and begin whisking in the butter, one cube at a time, until it has all been incorporated. Season with salt and the remainder of the truffle slices. Set aside in a warm spot until ready to serve.

Basil & Roasted Garlic Smashed Potatoes

I can't imagine going a week, or even a day, without cooking potatoes. I usually use red potatoes but a great variation is the Yukon Gold potato, due to its wonderful creamy texture. For me, the rule is: thin-skinned potato—no peeling!

— Judy

Serves 6

1	whole bulb garlic	1
3 lbs.	red potatoes	1.4 kg
2 Tbsp.	butter	30 mL
¾ cup	half-and-half cream	180 mL
1 Tbsp.	fresh basil, chopped coarsely	15 mL
	salt and freshly ground black pepper to taste	

Place the whole garlic bulb on a baking sheet and bake at 350°F (175°C) for 45 minutes. Remove from the oven, cut the top off and gently squeeze the cloves out.

Cut each potato into 8 pieces. Place them in a pot of cold water and bring to a boil. Continue boiling for 20 minutes, or until the potatoes are tender. Drain and return the potatoes to the pot. Stir lightly over low heat to make sure there is no water remaining.

Mash the potatoes with a potato masher. Add the garlic, butter and cream, still using the masher to incorporate all the ingredients. Finally add the basil, salt and pepper to taste. Serve immediately.

Portobello Mushroom & Asiago Cheese Potatoes:
While the potatoes are cooking, melt 1 Tbsp. (15 mL) butter in a frying pan over medium-high heat. Add 1 chopped Portobello mushroom and sauté for about 5 minutes. Set aside. Grate 1/2 cup (120 mL) Asiago cheese. Once the potatoes have been mashed and seasoned, stir in the mushrooms and cheese. Mix well and serve immediately.

Caramelized Onion & Dried Cranberry Potatoes

Serves 6

3 lbs.	red potatoes	1.4 kg
5 Tbsp.	butter	75 mL
1	large onion, finely diced	1
1 Tbsp.	sugar	15 mL
3 Tbsp.	dried cranberries	45 mL
½ tsp.	fresh thyme	2.5 mL
¾ cup	half-and-half cream	180 mL
	salt and freshly ground black pepper to taste	

Cut each potato into 8 pieces. Place them in a pot of cold water and bring to a boil. Continue boiling for 20 minutes, or until the potatoes are tender.

While the potatoes are cooking, melt 3 Tbsp. (45 mL) butter in a frying pan over medium-high heat. Add the onion and sugar and cook, stirring occasionally, until the onion is browned, about 10 to 15 minutes.

Add the cranberries and thyme and cook for another 3 minutes. Set aside.

Once the potatoes are cooked, drain off the water. Stir lightly over low heat to make sure there is no water remaining. Mash the potatoes with a potato masher, then add the remaining butter and the cream, blending thoroughly with the masher. Stir in the cranberry mixture and season with salt and pepper to taste.

This dish is perfect with roast Cornish game hen or roast pork. The secret to its success is to serve it with something that can complement its sweetness.

— Judy

Potato Gratin with Brie Cheese

*This gratin is perfect with roasted
lamb or chicken. If you're a blue
cheese fan, try substituting
Cambozola or Gorgonzola for the
Brie. I've seen people fight over
the last piece!*

— Pam

Serves 8

4 cups	whole milk	1 L
½ cup	whipping cream or Crème Fraîche (see page 216)	120 mL
6 oz.	Brie cheese, peeled and sliced	170 g
4 Tbsp.	unsalted butter	60 mL
4 lbs.	russet potatoes, peeled and thinly sliced	2 kg
	salt and freshly ground black pepper to taste	

Place the milk, cream and cheese in a saucepan over medium heat. Scald the milk, stirring occasionally.

Butter a 9- x 13-inch (23- x 33-cm) baking dish with 1 Tbsp. (15 mL) of the butter. Layer half the potatoes in the pan and season with salt and pepper. Add the remaining potatoes and pour the hot milk-cheese mixture over all. Season again with salt and pepper and dot with the remaining butter.

Preheat the oven to 350ºF (175ºC). Bake, uncovered, for 1 hour, until golden brown on top.

Cooking Beans

Beans are easy to cook but they take time. Canned beans are fine for refried beans, purées or when you're pressed for time, but beans cooked from scratch have a texture that's hard to beat. Canned beans tend to be high in sodium, so should be well rinsed before using.

The time it takes to cook dried beans will vary, depending on how dry they are. Put the beans in a big pot and add enough cold water to cover them by several inches (about 10 cm). Soak overnight, drain, and add fresh water before cooking.

To quick-soak, cover the beans with cold water in a pot, bring to a boil and boil hard for 2 minutes. Cover the pot, remove from the heat and let stand for 1 hour. Drain the beans and proceed with cooking.

Cover the presoaked beans with lots of water (at least an inch (2.5 cm) over the beans) and simmer, partly covered, for 1 to 2 hours.

Don't salt beans when you start cooking them. Salt can leave beans tough. Wait until the beans are partially cooked (about 45 minutes) before adding salt. Use 1 Tbsp. salt per cup (15 mL/240 mL) of beans. When done, the beans will be creamy inside and the skins will break when you blow on a bean in a spoon.

— Cinda Chavich

Luscious Beans with Asparagus, Leeks & Vanilla

Serves 6 to 8

3 Tbsp.	butter	45 mL
	zest of 1 lime	
3	1-inch (2.5-cm) pieces vanilla beans, split into quarters lengthwise and seeds scraped out	3
3	leeks, cut in thick slices	3
1 Tbsp.	lime juice	15 mL
½ cup	whipping cream or chicken stock	120 mL
	salt to taste	
1 cup	chicken stock	240 mL
2 lbs.	asparagus	900 g
½ lb.	dried pinto beans, cooked (see page 154)	250 g

Gently heat the butter and add the lime zest. Cook for about 2 minutes without allowing the lime zest to brown. Add the vanilla bean and leeks and sauté until the leeks are softened, about 10 to 15 minutes. Add the remaining ingredients except the asparagus and beans and simmer for 30 minutes.

Add the asparagus and cook for another 5 minutes. Toss with the cooked beans and heat through. Serve immediately.

I love taking familiar flavours out of context so that most people are left puzzled by the taste sensation. It is the food equivalent of bait and switch. Vanilla is great for that—used in a savoury context it will intrigue your guests and the flavour hints at sweetness without the "sweet." The whipping cream is optional, but it elevates this bean dish to the sublime.

— Gail

Warmed Lentils Dressed with Walnut Oil Vinaigrette

I have lost count of the number of times people have gone on and on about not liking lentils, then they try a spoonful of these lentils and their food prejudice is knocked down. Nuts and lentils are always a natural combination, both for taste and nutrition. Use any type of lentil you like, as long as it still has its jacket on so that the lentils remain intact and don't turn into a pot of mush.

— Gail

Serves 6 to 8

1	spicy sausage (optional)	1
4	slices bacon, finely chopped (optional)	4
	olive oil	
1	medium onion, chopped	1
4	cloves garlic, minced	4
2	red peppers, chopped	2
3	pods star anise	3
½ cup	chopped parsley	120 mL
½ cup	corn kernels, frozen or canned	120 mL
⅓ cup	chopped green onions	80 mL
2 cups	green or brown lentils, uncooked	480 mL
4 cups	chicken stock	1 L
¼ cup	red wine vinegar	60 mL
¼ cup	walnut oil	60 mL
	salt and freshly ground black pepper to taste	

If using sausage, bake or grill it until cooked through, then cut it into small chunks and set aside.

If using bacon, cook it until crisp, then remove from the pan and set aside.

Drain off some of the bacon fat if excessive, and add enough olive oil to cover the bottom of the pan. Sauté the onion, garlic, red pepper and star anise over medium heat until slightly soft. Add the parsley, corn, green onions and lentils, and stir to coat.

Add the stock and bring to a boil, then turn down the heat and gently simmer uncovered until the lentils are soft but not mushy, about 30 minutes. Do not let the lentils become dry; add more water or stock as required.

When the lentils are done, add the cooked bacon and sausage, if desired, the vinegar and walnut oil and simmer with the lid off. Continue cooking gently until the liquids have been absorbed. Season with salt and pepper and serve.

Recommended wine:
fruity grenache or New World gamay

Vegetarian Chickpea Curry with Flatbread

Serves 8 as an entrée or 12 as part of a buffet

½ cup	vegetable oil	120 mL
2	large onions, chopped	2
¾ tsp.	ground ginger	3.75 mL
1 Tbsp.	ground coriander	15 mL
½ Tbsp.	ground turmeric	7.5 mL
1 Tbsp.	ground cumin	15 mL
¼ tsp.	ground cinnamon	1.2 mL
½ tsp.	cayenne	2.5 mL
2–3	bay leaves	2–3
1 cup	water	240 mL
2	28-oz. (784-mL) cans chickpeas, drained and rinsed	2
2	tomatoes, chopped, for garnish	2
1	onion, finely chopped, for garnish	1
	Yeasted Flatbread or Naan (see page 191)	

Heat the oil over medium heat in a large sauté pan. Add the onions and cook until they become soft and transparent. Stir in the spices, bay leaves and water until it is well mixed and begins to bubble. Add the chickpeas and cook over medium heat until very fragrant, approximately 20 to 30 minutes.

If the curry becomes too thick, add water while cooking. It should be thick enough to be scooped up with the flatbread. Remove the bay leaves. Serve "communal style" with the chopped tomatoes, onions and flatbread on the side.

I attended a cooking class presented by Shakeh's Kitchen at the old Benkris cooking school in Kensington years ago. At that time, I wasn't interested in vegetarian food, but when I tasted Shakeh's chickpea curry, I began to gain an appreciation for meatless cooking. Unfortunately, I moved a few times and my recipe disappeared. The following is my best recreation of that wonderful curry.

— Janet

breakfast, brunch or lunch

Pear Vanilla Honey

If you like pears, you'll love this spread on warm, buttered whole-grain toast. I also use it to sweeten vinaigrettes for fall salads that feature pears.

— Pam

Makes seven ½-pint (250-mL) jars

7 ½ lbs.	medium ripe pears	3.4 kg
1 cup	honey	240 mL
7	vanilla beans	7

Wash and chop the pears. Heat in a stainless-steel pot over medium-high, crushing with a masher to release juice. Bring to a boil, cover and reduce the heat to low. Stirring occasionally, simmer until the pears are soft, 20 to 30 minutes.

Press through a sieve to yield 10 cups (2.5 L). Purée in batches in a food processor.

Return to the pot and bring to a boil. Add the honey and bring to a boil again. Simmer 20 minutes, or until the pear honey mounds slightly on a spoon.

Sterilize jars, place 1 vanilla bean in each, and pour in the hot mixture up to ¾ inch (2 cm) from the top. Seal with sterilized, hot rings and lids. Store in a refrigerator for up to 1 year.

roasted garlic & pepper soup with basil oil (page 53)

prosciutto-wrapped endive (page 146)

chicken breast brochettes with moroccan chermoula (page 85),
and cinnamon-scented couscous (page 142)

tenderloin for two with blue cheese butter (page 98)
and basil & roasted garlic smashed potatoes (page 152)

Pineapple-Melon Ginger Jam

Makes eight to ten 8-oz. (250-mL) jars

2 lbs.	ripe honeydew melon (ripe but not overripe), peeled, seeded and chopped	900 g
1 lb.	pineapple	450 g
1	egg-sized piece of ginger, peeled and slightly crushed	1
3	lemons, juice of three; zest of one	3
1 ½ lbs.	sugar	675 g

In a large confiture pan (large, heavy and broader than deep), simmer the fruit, ginger, lemon juice and zest, as well as the lemon rinds and pips. The rinds and pips can be put in a cheesecloth bag to expedite removal. Simmer only until the fruit is starting to break down. Remove the ginger, lemon rinds and pips, squeezing out the juice.

Slowly add the sugar and stir to dissolve over medium heat. Don't bring to a boil until the sugar is completely dissolved, then bring to a rolling boil and cook rapidly until the fruit sets. The liquid will begin to sheet off a metal spoon. I also put a saucer in the freezer and after about 15 to 20 minutes I begin to test for a set. Put a spoonful of the boiling jam on the saucer and return it to the freezer for a couple of minutes or less. With your finger, push into the jam. If it wrinkles and doesn't fill in after your finger pulls away, it's a go.

Take the pot off the heat and allow to sit for 15 minutes so the fruit doesn't all float to the top of your jars. Fill jars according to the manufacturer's instructions.

The pineapple makes this unusual jam even more interesting. However, if you prefer, you can omit the pineapple and use 3 lbs. (1.35 kg) melon. I don't use pectin, preferring a looser spread.

— Ellen

Citrus Fruit & Champagne Terrine

A Champagne brunch would be enhanced by this refreshing terrine. Set out slices on a serving platter or let your guests cut their own slice with a sharp, thin-bladed knife. If you want to vary the fruit in this dish, it's simplest to avoid figs, ginger, papaya, pineapple, kiwi fruit and honey-dew melon. All contain an enzyme that inhibits the setting action of gelatin. The solution, if these fruits are what you really want, is to cook them first to a temperature of 185°F (85°C), which will kill the problem enzymes. If you do not have a terrine mold with hinged sides that fold down, you can use ramekins for individual portions instead, and serve them without unmolding the contents.

— dee

Serves 6 to 10

2	packages of unflavoured gelatin	2
1 bottle	Champagne, at room temperature	1 bottle
1 cup	sugar	240 mL
1 cup	green and red seedless grapes, halved	240 mL
1	orange, segmented	1
1	blood orange, segmented	1
1	pink grapefruit, segmented	1
1	lemon, segmented	1
1	lime, segmented	1
1 tsp.	fresh thyme leaves	5 mL

Sprinkle the gelatin on 1 cup (240 mL) of Champagne, then gently heat just enough to thoroughly melt the gelatin. Allow the temperature to drop until the aspic becomes syrupy. If it gets stiff, gently reheat to melt. (Do not boil.)

Gently heat the remaining Champagne with the sugar. Stir in the melted gelatin and its liquid. Pour 1/3 of the mixture into a lined mold and let set, covered, in the fridge for 45 to 60 minutes.

Add 1/3 of the grapes and citrus segments and another 1/3 of the liquid. Let set for 45 to 60 minutes.

Add another 1/3 of the grapes and citrus segments and the remaining liquid. Let set for 45 to 60 minutes, then top with the remaining grapes and citrus segments. Chill well, covered. Slice with a hot, wet knife to serve.

Swiss Muesli

Serves 4

with inspiration from Bircher muesli

1 cup	organic rolled oats	240 mL
1 cup	water	240 mL
½ cup	plain organic yogurt	120 mL
½ cup	grated green apple	120 mL
1	banana, chopped	1
1 Tbsp.	chopped nuts	15 mL
1 Tbsp.	sunflower seeds	15 mL
	honey to taste	
½ cup	raspberries (or any fresh berries)	120 mL

Soak the oats in water overnight, in a covered bowl. In the morning, stir in the remaining ingredients except the berries, which should be scattered on top.

Winter Muesli: Use ½ cup (120 mL) of raisins, chopped prunes or chopped dried apricots in lieu of berries.

Fresh and delicious, I love muesli in the morning or as a snack. It will keep in the refrigerator for several days and makes an easy and colourful addition to a brunch table.

— Rhondda

Yogurt

Organic yogurt tastes wonderful—and it contains live beneficial bacteria that improve digestion and destroy disease-causing bacteria. If you can't get organic yogurt, non-organic ones may also have live bacteria; check that the label states it contains active bacterial culture.

— Rhondda Siebens

Recommended wine:
light New Zealand or South African
sauvignon blanc, or bubbly

Garden-Fresh Frittata

This recipe lets you use what is fresh, in season, or in your pantry. You can add or change ingredients to suit your tastes. Try varying the cheeses and herbs, or try different vegetables, such as fresh peas, asparagus or corn, or olives. It's a perfect dish for a brunch buffet.

— Rosemary

Serves 8

2	small jars marinated artichokes	2
1	small onion, chopped fine	1
1	clove garlic, minced	1
⅓ cup	red pepper, chopped	80 mL
4	eggs	4
¼ cup	bread crumbs or cornmeal	60 mL
¼ tsp.	freshly ground black pepper	1.2 mL
¼ tsp.	oregano	1.2 mL
2 Tbsp.	fresh parsley, chopped	30 mL
½ cup	cream	120 mL
¼ lb.	cheddar cheese, grated	115 g
¼ lb.	Parmesan cheese, grated	115 g
¼ lb.	Gruyère cheese, grated	115 g

Drain the oil from one jar of artichokes into a frying pan. Discard the oil from the other jar. Chop the artichokes and set aside. Sauté the onion, garlic and red pepper in the oil over medium-high for about 5 minutes, stirring frequently.

Preheat the oven to 350°F (175°C). In a large bowl, beat the eggs just until frothy. Add the bread crumbs or cornmeal, pepper, oregano, parsley and cream. Add the cooked onion and pepper, the artichokes and ⅔ of the cheese.

Put the mixture into a greased 10-inch (25-cm) round pie plate or 8-inch (20-cm) square cake pan. Sprinkle with the remaining cheese. Bake for 20 to 30 minutes until set. Serve warm or at room temperature.

Cappuccino Eggs

Serves 1

3	eggs	3
¼ cup	milk	60 mL
¼ cup	chèvre or your favourite grated hard cheese	60 mL
1	green onion, chopped	1
	salt and freshly ground black pepper to taste	

In a stainless steel container (like the ones commonly used to heat milk on a cappuccino machine) combine all ingredients. Steam with the steaming nozzle for 30 seconds or until the egg mixture froths briefly. Enjoy with a cappuccino, of course!

This refers to the cooking method, not the flavour! Just another fun and speedy way to use your cappuccino machine—think of the fluffiest scrambled eggs imaginable.

— Rhondda

Savoury Brioche Bread Pudding

Bread pudding was never my favourite until I was inspired by Georgeanne Brennan's book, Potager, to try this as a side dish for poultry. By adding meat, it becomes a hearty meal in itself. Great for brunch, lunch or a spring dinner

— Rosemary.

Serves 6 to 8

3 cups	milk	720 mL
12–15	slices day-old brioche (or any flavourful bread you like)	12–15
5	eggs	5
1 tsp.	salt	5 mL
1 tsp.	pepper	5 mL
1 lb.	asparagus, ends trimmed	450 g
½ cup	Swiss-type cheese (I like Jarlsberg), grated	120 mL
½ cup	Parmesan cheese, grated	120 mL
½ cup	soft flavourful cheese, such as mascarpone, chèvre or Cambozola	120 mL
½ cup	fresh herbs, chopped (any assortment—chives, oregano, tarragon, parsley, thyme, basil)	120 mL

Butter a 3-quart (3-L) ovensafe dish. Pour ½ cup (120 mL) milk into the dish. Put a layer of bread slices on top.

Beat the eggs, salt, pepper and the remaining 2 ½ cups (600 mL) milk until blended.

Sprinkle the layer of bread slices with ⅓ of the asparagus, ⅓ of the cheeses and ½ of the herbs. Repeat the layering with more bread, ⅓ of the asparagus, ⅓ of the cheeses and the rest of the herbs. Add a final layer of the remaining bread, asparagus and cheese. Pour the milk-egg mixture over all. Press down to make sure all the bread is moistened. Let sit for 20 minutes.

Preheat the oven to 350°F (175°C). Bake for 45 minutes until golden brown and a knife inserted in the middle of the pudding comes out clean.

Bread Pudding with Chicken or Ham: For a main course, add 1 ½ cups (360 mL) chopped ham or smoked chicken with the asparagus layers.

Gingerbread Pancakes with Lemon Sauce

Serves 4 to 6

1 ⅓ cups	all-purpose flour	320 mL
1 tsp.	baking powder	5 mL
¼ tsp.	baking soda	1.2 mL
½ tsp.	kosher salt	2.5 mL
½ tsp.	ground ginger	2.5 mL
1 tsp.	ground cinnamon	5 mL
1	egg	1
1 ¼ cups	milk	300 mL
¼ cup	molasses	60 mL
3 Tbsp.	vegetable oil	45 mL
½ recipe	Lemon Sauce	½ recipe

Mix the dry ingredients in a medium bowl. In a separate bowl, mix the egg and milk, then stir in the molasses and add the oil. Add the wet ingredients to the dry ingredients and stir until just combined.

Heat a non-stick pan or griddle on high, then turn it down to medium-high. Lightly oil the pan, then spoon on the batter with a ¼ to ½ cup (60 to 120 mL) ladle. Flip each pancake once bubbles form, turning only once. Serve warm with butter and Lemon Sauce.

Lemon Sauce

This recipe makes enough for a double batch of pancakes.

Makes about 1 ½ cups (360 mL)

½ cup	sugar	120 mL
1 Tbsp.	cornstarch	15 mL
pinch	nutmeg	pinch
1 cup	hot water	240 mL
2 Tbsp.	butter	30 mL
½ tsp.	lemon rind, grated	2.5 mL
2 Tbsp.	lemon juice (or to taste)	30 mL

Mix the sugar, cornstarch and nutmeg in a medium saucepan. Gradually mix in the water. Cook over medium heat until the mixture is thick and clear, about 15 minutes. Stir in the butter, lemon rind and lemon juice. Keep the sauce warm while you make the pancakes.

This is an all-time favourite with kids, but it appears that there are many "big kids" who cherish the memory of warm gingerbread from their youth as well. My friend Shannon Daly shared this recipe with me after my son experienced them during a weekend sleepover. These pancakes become quite dark due to the molasses. They are tasty cold, and you can spread the lemon sauce on them straight from the fridge as a quick snack.

— Janet

Apple & Gorgonzola Beignets

These heavenly fritters are a bit labour intensive, but you can make the crêpes and the filling ahead of time. Make sure your oil is just right—too hot and you'll burn the beignets, not hot enough and they will be oily. It's worth having an oil thermometer to be sure.

— Ellen

Makes 16 to 20

1 recipe	Ginger Crêpes (see page 218)	1 recipe
¼ cup	buttermilk	60 mL
4	small Braeburn apples	4
1 Tbsp.	unsalted butter	15 mL
1 Tbsp.	brown sugar	15 mL
¼ cup	apple juice or cider	60 mL
½ lb.	Gorgonzola cheese	225 g
	light vegetable oil	
	cornstarch	
	icing sugar, for dusting	

Prepare the crêpe recipe and divide in half. Make crêpes with half the recipe and thin the other half with the buttermilk.

Peel, core and roughly chop the apples. Melt the butter in a heavy pan on medium-high heat, add the apples and sprinkle with the brown sugar. Allow to cook for 5 minutes or so, without stirring, to caramelize. Add the juice or cider and stir. Continue to cook until the liquid is absorbed and the apples are golden. Set aside to cool completely.

To fill the beignets, lay a crêpe out on the counter and put a small spoonful each of the applesauce and Gorgonzola in the centre. Fold the crêpe into the centre like a small square package, with the same number of layers of crêpe on each side of the bundle to prevent breakage while deep-frying.

Put 2 to 3 inches (5 to 7.5 cm) oil in a deep, heavy pan and heat to 350ºF (175ºC). Dust each beignet lightly with cornstarch, brushing off any excess. Dip each beignet in the reserved crêpe batter, shake off any excess and carefully place in the hot oil. Only cook a few at a time; don't crowd the pan. Fry them for about 5 minutes on each side or until golden and crispy. Remove from the oil with tongs or a slotted spoon, let drain and keep warm in a 275ºF (135ºC) oven while you cook the rest of the fritters.

Dust with icing sugar and serve warm.

Hazelnut & Chocolate-Wrapped Figs in Puff Pastry

Serves 8

1 cup	hazelnuts	240 mL
¼ lb.	Valrhona dark chocolate	115 g
⅓ cup	sugar	80 mL
1 lb.	puff pastry	450 g
8	fresh figs	8

Preheat the oven to 375ºF (190ºC). Place the hazelnuts on a cookie sheet and roast them in the oven for about 15 to 20 minutes. They are done when you begin to smell the nut aroma. Don't leave the kitchen while the hazelnuts are roasting! The minute you do they will burn, and you'll have to start again. When they are done, place them on a towel and rub as much of the skins off as possible.

Put the hazelnuts into a food processor along with the chocolate and sugar, and pulse together.

Roll the puff pastry out to a scant ¼ inch (.6 cm) thickness. Cut into 8 square pieces and distribute the chocolate and hazelnut mixture equally on top of each square. Place a fig in the middle and wrap the pastry up around the top to form a sort of twist.

Bake at 375ºC (190ºC) for about 15 to 20 minutes or until nicely browned. Serve while still hot.

A spectacular brunch dish. You can buy prepared puff pastry at the supermarket. However, I usually go to my favourite French bakery and ask to buy some of their dough, as it is usually of a higher quality than the supermarket variety. When fresh figs are not available, try cherries, sliced mangoes or pears.

— Gail

Puff Pastry–Wrapped Pears on Arugula with Pecans & St. Agur

This wonderful brunch item also stands alone very well as a lunch course—I've even served it as a dessert. The pears can be baked in advance and served at room temperature.

— Shelley

Serves 4

8 cups	water	2 L
2 cups	sugar	480 mL
1	lemon, washed and cut into quarters	1
1	orange, washed and cut into quarters	1
1	vanilla bean, split and seeds scraped out	1
4	medium-size, not overly ripe pears	4
1	package frozen puff pastry	1
1	egg yolk	1
1 Tbsp.	milk	15 mL
½ cup	St. Agur or similar blue cheese, crumbled	120 mL
½ cup	toasted pecans (see page 171)	120 mL
¼ lb.	arugula, cleaned and trimmed	115 g
2 Tbsp.	pecan or hazelnut oil	30 mL
1 Tbsp.	poaching liquid from pears	15 mL

Place the water, sugar, lemon, orange and split vanilla bean with its seeds in a pot.

Peel the pears and, using a melon baller, scoop out the core area from the bottom of the pear. Place the pears in the pot and simmer on medium heat uncovered for 15 to 20 minutes, or until the pears do not resist piercing by a sharp knife. Using a slotted spoon, carefully remove the pears and place on a cooling rack. Reserve the poaching liquid.

Roll out the puff pastry to ¼ inch (.6 cm) thickness. Cut 4 squares approximately 4 x 4 inches (10 x 10 cm).

Whisk together the egg yolk and milk and lightly brush each pastry square.

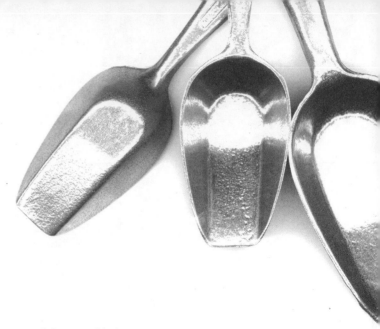

Stuff the centre of each pear with some of the crumbled cheese and a few pecans, reserving some cheese and pecans for garnish. Place each stuffed pear in the centre of a pastry square. Pull one corner up toward the top of the pear, then pull up the corner next to it and slightly overlap the dough. Press to stick the pieces together. Continue until the pears are securely wrapped in the pastry, then brush the outside of each pear with the remaining yolk-milk mixture and refrigerate for 10 minutes.

Preheat the oven to 425ºF (220ºC). Place the pears on a baking sheet and bake on the centre rack of the oven for 15 to 20 minutes, until the dough is golden brown. Remove and let cool slightly on a rack.

Toss the arugula, pecan oil and the remaining cheese and pecans with the poaching liquid from the pears. Divide the salad between 4 plates and serve a baked pear on top.

Toasting Nuts

If you want an even, monochromatic tone to your toasted nuts, bake them in a single layer at 300ºF (150ºC) without stirring until they are a golden brown. Time will vary, depending on the size of the tray and amount of nuts; a scant half-cup (125 mL) will toast nicely in 5 minutes, but a larger volume may take up to 20 minutes. If you like a variegated collection of tones, set the oven higher and stir the nuts frequently so the outside edges are moved into the centre of the tray. Check them every few minute. By the time your nose alerts you to over-browned nuts, it is too late to rescue them.

—dee Hobsbawn-Smith

Pan Bagna

Serves 2

4	ripe Roma tomatoes, quartered	4
1	small purple onion, diced	1
¼	cucumber, thinly sliced	¼
¼ cup	Niçoise olives, pitted and coarsely chopped	60 mL
2 Tbsp.	fresh parsley, chopped	30 mL
1	4.7-oz. (133-g) can white tuna, well drained	1
	salt and freshly ground black pepper to taste	
	olive oil to taste	
	balsamic vinegar to taste	
2	6-inch (15-cm) round loaves of crusty bread	2

Combine the tomatoes, onion, cucumber, olives, parsley, tuna, salt and pepper in a bowl. Drizzle lightly with olive oil and balsamic vinegar.

Cut the top ⅓ off the loaves and remove a large enough portion of bread from the inside to hold the salad. Drizzle a small amount of olive oil into the bread and pour the salad into the two loaves. Put the top of the bread back on and enjoy!

Panini Sandwich of Cognac Pâté, Grilled Mushrooms & Cambozola

Serves 2

1	Portobello mushroom, sliced	1
1 Tbsp.	olive oil	15 mL
2	panini buns	2
1 recipe	Cognac Pâté (see page 174)	1 recipe
½ lb.	Cambozola cheese, thinly sliced	225 g
2 Tbsp.	Sun-Dried Tomato Dressing (see page 174)	30 mL

Toss the mushroom slices in a bowl with olive oil. Cook on a hot grill or in a sauté pan on medium-high heat for about 5 minutes.

Cut the panini buns in half and spread the pâté on one side. Top with mushroom slices and Cambozola cheese. Drizzle the dressing over top and replace the top of the panini bun.

The best and simplest way to cook panini is in a sandwich grill. But if you haven't got one, you can fake it quite well. Butter the bottom of the buns and set them in a preheated frying pan on medium heat. Put a large, heavy pot on top of the buns with heavy cans, a rock or other heavy object in it to compress the panini. When the buns are lightly browned on one side, about 3 to 5 minutes, remove the pot. Butter the top of the buns, flip them over and replace the pot and rock. Cook another 3 to 5 minutes until the cheese is melted.

Alternatively, you can compress the buns with your hand, place the buns on a baking sheet and bake in a 350ºF (175ºC) oven for 5 minutes. This misses the grilled flavour of the buns, though, and you must be careful the buns don't overcook or they will be dry.

Cut the buns in half and serve immediately.

The succulent flavours all melting together make a heavenly lunch. If you don't want to make the pâté, some great pâtés are available in deli stores! Cambozola is a German cheese similar to Camembert, with a streak of Gorgonzola running through it.

— Judy

Cognac Pâté

Makes 1/2 lb. (225 g)

1 Tbsp.	butter	15 mL
1	shallot, finely chopped	1
1	clove garlic, minced	1
1/3 lb.	chicken livers	150 g
1/4 cup	cognac or brandy	60 mL
1 tsp.	flour	5 mL
1/4 cup	whipping cream	60 mL
1 tsp.	fresh thyme	5 mL
	salt and freshly ground black pepper to taste	

In a frying pan over medium heat, melt the butter. Add the shallot and garlic, cook for 2 to 3 minutes until soft, then add the chicken livers and cook for 5 minutes. Spoon the cognac in carefully, as it is flammable, and let it reduce until only about a teaspoonful (5 mL) remains.

Add the flour and cook for 2 minutes, stirring lightly. Then add the cream and bring to a boil, stirring lightly to make sure you include any bits that are stuck to the bottom of the pan. Turn the heat down and simmer for 3 minutes. Add the thyme, salt and pepper.

Put all the ingredients into a blender and purée. Scrape into a small mold or bowl, adding coarse-ground pepper to the top if you wish. Refrigerate until you are ready to use it.

Sun-Dried Tomato Dressing

Try the leftover dressing in a pasta salad or on a grilled chicken baguette sandwich.

Makes 1/2 cup (120 mL)

3	sun-dried tomatoes	3
1/2	green onion	1/2
1 Tbsp.	balsamic vinegar	15 mL
1/2 tsp.	Dijon mustard	2.5 mL
1/4 cup	mayonnaise	60 mL
1 Tbsp.	buttermilk	15 mL
	salt and freshly ground black pepper to taste	

Soak the tomatoes in 1/2 cup (120 mL) hot water for 5 minutes. Drain, reserving the liquid for soups.

Put the tomatoes, green onion, vinegar and mustard into a blender and purée. Add the mayonnaise, buttermilk, salt and pepper. Keep in the refrigerator.

Focaccia with Your Choice of Toppings

Makes one 12- x 17-inch (30- x 43-cm) pan

For the dough:

3 ½ cups	water	840 mL
2 Tbsp.	yeast	30 mL
1 ½ Tbsp.	sugar	22 mL
¼ cup	olive oil	60 mL
1 ½ Tbsp.	salt	22 mL
5 cups	bread flour	1.2 L
	cornmeal, for dusting pan	

Mix 1 cup (240 mL) hot tap water with the yeast and sugar. Let sit for 10 minutes until bubbly. Mix in the remaining 2 ½ cups (600 mL) water, oil, salt and half the flour. You may use a dough mixer or blend it by hand with a wooden spoon.

Gradually mix in the rest of the flour. You may not need all of the flour. The dough should be very soft, almost runny. Let the dough rise for 45 minutes.

Rub a large baking sheet with olive oil, then sprinkle the sheet with cornmeal. Oil your hands and push the dough out to the corners of the baking sheet. Now you are ready to put on the topping of your choice.

Once you've added your toppings, bake the focaccia in a preheated 375ºF (190ºC) oven for 35 minutes, until golden brown around the edges. Let sit 10 minutes before cutting.

Focaccia with Salt and Herbs: Spread a little olive oil over the dough, then sprinkle on a little sea salt, freshly ground black pepper, dried herbs such as oregano, thyme and basil, and grated Parmesan.

See page 176 for more toppings.

This dough is very easy and versatile. The suggested toppings offer endless possibilities for variation.

— Rosemary

Focaccia with Pesto, Herbs and Cheese: Spread a layer of sauce over the dough—you can use a pesto made of basil, red peppers or cilantro, or a simple tomato sauce. Top the sauce with fresh herbs and grated cheese. It is best to use a combination of cheeses, with some that will melt as well as harder grating cheeses. Cheeses that melt well are chèvre, Monterey, fruiliano and mozzarella. Cheeses that grate and add flavour are Parmigiano, Romano, hard jack, Jarlsberg and Gruyère. Soft cheeses such as Gorgonzola, Cambozola and goat cheese can be cut in small pieces and dropped on the top.

Focaccia with Sautéed or Roasted Vegetables and Cheese: The sky's the limit on possible combinations. Use any vegetables that you like, such as peppers, onions, eggplant, squash, fennel, mushrooms, potatoes, tomatoes or asparagus. We usually roast or sauté the vegetables first. After you have partially cooked them, cut them into small pieces and sprinkle them on the dough. Top with herbs and cheese. For an unusual combination, try fresh peas, fresh sage, Cambozola cheese and sautéed onions.

Truffle-Scented Focaccia with Taleggio

Makes three 8-inch (20-cm) rounds

1 recipe	Pizza Dough (see page 179)	1 recipe
	flour and cornmeal for dusting	
1 lb.	Taleggio cheese, thinly sliced	450 g
1 Tbsp.	white truffle oil	15 mL
	sea salt to taste	

Preheat the oven to 450°F (230°C). If using a pizza stone, place it in the oven for at least 40 minutes. Divide the dough into 3 pieces and shape each into rounds. Work or roll into 8-inch (20-cm) rounds and dimple the top with your fingertips. Let the dough rise slightly (for about 20 minutes) on a cornmeal-dusted baking sheet, then place in the oven for about 10 minutes or until the top is golden brown.

Remove from the oven and slice each round horizontally, using a bread knife. Spread the sliced cheese on the bottom layer and replace the top. Do this quickly so the bread does not cool down. Place the rounds back in the oven for about 2 minutes, just to warm the cheese. Remove them from the oven, drizzle the truffle oil over the top and sprinkle with sea salt. Slice into thin wedges.

I had a version of this pizza for lunch at a restaurant run by Pino Luongo down in the basement of the ever trendy Barney's department store in New York City. I remember wondering whether it was worth giving up our shopping time when we were told it would be at least a half-hour wait, but also remember leaving thinking it was the best lunch I'd ever had. That says a lot for a salad and a pizza.

The cheese used was Robiola, beautifully smooth and fragrant. On a mission when I got home to find the cheese in local Italian hangouts, I was told it was unpasteurized and much too fragile for transportation. Not to be discouraged, I tried to recreate it with Taleggio, another creamy, tangy Italian cheese. I don't think it's as good as the original, but here is a very acceptable variation.

— Karen

Pissaladiere

This is a pizza from southern France. I first tasted this bread while I was working at a bakery café in San Francisco named Tart to Tart. We made pissaladiere every day for lunch. As with pizza, you can take liberties with the toppings. Since I don't care for anchovies, I leave them out even though they are a traditional ingredient. You may substitute any pizza dough for the focaccia, as long as it is thick enough. It should be more of a bread crust than a flat, thin crust.

— Rosemary

Makes 24 to 48 pieces

1 recipe	Focaccia Dough (see page 175)	1 recipe
6 Tbsp.	olive oil	90 mL
2 Tbsp.	butter	30 mL
6	onions, thinly sliced	6
2	bay leaves	2
1 Tbsp.	sugar	15 mL
1 tsp.	salt	5 mL
2 Tbsp.	white wine	30 mL
¼ cup	cornmeal	60 mL
½ cup	Dijon mustard	120 mL
3–4	tomatoes, sliced and drained	3–4
	salt and freshly ground black pepper to taste	
¼ cup	mixed oregano and thyme, minced	60 mL
1 cup	Niçoise or kalamata olives	240 mL
½ cup	mixed Asiago and Gruyère cheese, grated	120 mL

Prepare the focaccia dough and let it rise while you make the toppings.

In a large frying pan or saucepan with a cover, combine 4 Tbsp. (60 mL) of olive oil and the butter over high heat. When hot, add the onions, bay leaves, sugar and salt. Cover, reduce the heat to low and cook for 10 minutes.

Uncover and stir. Increase the heat to medium and cook another 10 minutes, stirring occasionally. Increase the heat to medium-high and cook, stirring, until the onions are golden brown, about 10 more minutes. Stir in the wine and remove from the heat.

Preheat the oven to 400°F (200°C). Sprinkle a 12- x 17-inch (30- x 43-cm) pan with cornmeal. Spread the focaccia dough over the pan. Let sit 5 minutes. Gently spread the mustard over the dough, leaving a border around the edge. Spread the tomato slices on the dough and top with a little salt and pepper.

Remove the bay leaves from the onions and spread the onions over the tomatoes. Sprinkle $1/2$ the oregano and thyme over the onions, then top with the olives and cheese.

Bake 20 to 30 minutes, until golden and crisp around the edge. While still hot, drizzle the remaining 2 Tbsp. (30 mL) of olive oil and the remaining herbs over top. Serve hot or at room temperature.

Smoked Applewood Cheddar & Fuji Apple Pizza

Makes four 8-inch (20-cm) pizza rounds

For the dough:

1 Tbsp.	yeast	15 mL
1 ⅓ cups	warm water	320 mL
1 tsp.	granulated sugar	5 mL
1 Tbsp.	sea salt	15 mL
1 Tbsp.	olive oil	15 mL
3 cups	unbleached all-purpose flour	720 mL
	extra flour for dusting	

For the topping:

4 Tbsp.	roasted garlic paste (see page 16)	60 mL
3	Fuji apples, peeled and thinly sliced	3
½ lb.	smoked applewood cheddar, thinly sliced	225 g
1	bunch green onions, thinly sliced on the diagonal	1
	sea salt and freshly ground black pepper to taste	

People are always surprised when I tell them there are apples on the pizza. The combination of roasted garlic, cheese and apples is spectacular and far removed from red sauce and pepperoni pizzas. You can substitute plain white cheddar, but the layers of flavour will not be the same. The pizza dough recipe is adapted from a Wolfgang Puck recipe. It's the first pizza dough I ever tried to make—and the recipe I always come back to. You don't need an electric mixer to make the dough; just knead it by hand until the dough is smooth textured and elastic.

— Karen

To make the pizza dough, stir the yeast into the water and add sugar. Let stand until bubbly, about 10 minutes.

If mixing by hand, add the sea salt and olive oil, then stir in the flour gradually, until the dough is soft and pulls away from the side of the bowl.

If using an electric mixer, place 1 ½ cups (360 mL) flour in a mixer fitted with a dough hook. Add the salt and olive oil to the yeast mixture and mix into the flour. On medium speed, continue to add flour until the dough starts to pull away from the sides of the mixer. It should be smooth and elastic.

Place the dough in an oiled bowl and cover. Let rise in a warm place until doubled in size, about 1 hour. Punch down the dough, cover it again and let rise a second time until doubled in size, about 1 hour.

Preheat the oven to 450ºF (230ºC). Prepare a floured surface and cut the dough into 4 pieces. Roll out each piece into thin rounds, about 8 inches (20 cm) in diameter, and place on baking sheets lined with parchment paper. Spread garlic paste over each round and cover with apple slices. Top with slices of cheese and sprinkle with green onions, salt and pepper. Bake 10 to 12 minutes, until the crust is golden and the cheese is melted.

Recommended wine:
French marsanne/roussane or
fuller-bodied Italian pinot gris

Quesadilla Cake with Apple, Onion, Mint Pesto & Cambozola

I've always loved quesadillas, but never found a recipe that allowed me to make them ahead that had any holding power. Soggy is not where it's at! This idea works very well, as the grilling of the apples removes some moisture and grilling the tortillas gives them more body. Cook the onions well to remove as much liquid as possible. I like the mint pesto, but any pesto will work. If you want to substitute for the Cambozola, use a full-fat, easy-melting cheese such as Brie or Camembert. This cake also makes a great appetizer, cut in smaller wedges.

— Shelley

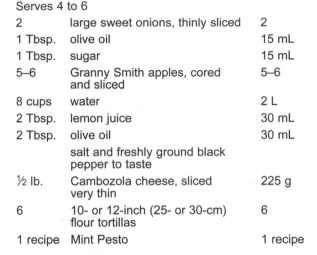

Serves 4 to 6

2	large sweet onions, thinly sliced	2
1 Tbsp.	olive oil	15 mL
1 Tbsp.	sugar	15 mL
5–6	Granny Smith apples, cored and sliced	5–6
8 cups	water	2 L
2 Tbsp.	lemon juice	30 mL
2 Tbsp.	olive oil	30 mL
	salt and freshly ground black pepper to taste	
½ lb.	Cambozola cheese, sliced very thin	225 g
6	10- or 12-inch (25- or 30-cm) flour tortillas	6
1 recipe	Mint Pesto	1 recipe

Cut the onions in half lengthwise, and remove the skin and the majority of the core. Slice the onions into long thin strips. Preheat a large sauté pan over medium-low heat and add the oil, then stir in the onions and sprinkle the sugar over top. Cook, stirring often, until the onions are dark golden brown, about 10 to 12 minutes. Set aside and cool.

Preheat a barbecue or grill to medium-high. Core the apples and slice into ¼ inch (.6 cm) thickness. Place the slices into the water with the lemon juice. Once all the apple slices are in the water, remove only what you can grill at one time. Dry the slices on a kitchen towel, then brush them with olive oil and season with salt and pepper. Grill the apples on both sides, but do not allow them to get too soft. Set them on a baking sheet to cool and continue the process with the remaining slices.

While the grill is still on, brush the oil lightly on both sides of the tortillas and grill each side lightly.

To assemble, place a tortilla on a work surface and spread 1 Tbsp. (15 mL) of the Mint Pesto evenly over the entire surface. Top with ⅕ of the apple slices (but do not overlap them), then with an even, single layer of onions followed by ⅕ of the cheese. Top with a tortilla. Repeat this process 4 more times and finish by laying the last tortilla on top. Press firmly down on the cake and put a large plate on top. Cover tightly with plastic wrap until ready to serve.

Cut into wedges and heat in a 425ºF (210ºC) oven until warmed through. Serve with a salsa that has lots of kick.

Mint Pesto

Makes about 1 cup (240 mL)

2 cups	fresh mint leaves, washed	480 mL
2	cloves garlic, roughly chopped	2
¼ cup	hazelnuts, toasted and cooled (see page 171)	60 mL
1 Tbsp.	fresh lemon juice	15 mL
½ cup	olive oil	120 mL
1 tsp.	sugar	5 mL
	salt and freshly ground black pepper to taste	

Place the mint leaves, garlic, hazelnuts and lemon juice in the bowl of a food processor. Begin to run the motor and slowly add the oil. Scrape down the sides of the bowl to incorporate all the mint into a paste. Season with the sugar, salt and pepper, then scrape into a bowl and set aside.

Portobello Mushroom Tart with Boursin & Asparagus

Here is the marriage of three fabulous flavours wrapped in a perfect package. The words divine and heavenly come quickly to mind.

— Judy

Serves 6

24	asparagus stalks	24
6	medium Portobello mushrooms	6
1	medium zucchini, thinly sliced	1
3	Roma tomatoes, thinly sliced	3
1 Tbsp.	fresh thyme, coarsely chopped	15 mL
	salt and and freshly ground black pepper to taste	
6 oz.	Boursin cheese	180 g
1 cup	balsamic vinegar	240 mL
6 cups	mesclun, loosely packed	1.5 L

Preheat the oven to 350ºF (175ºC). Set a pot of salted water on the stove to boil. Cut the asparagus stalks to the width of the mushrooms and set aside.

Remove the stems from the mushrooms and set the tops on a baking sheet ready to be filled. Place a layer of zucchini slices, then a layer of tomato slices on the mushrooms. Sprinkle the thyme, salt and pepper over the top.

Once the water is boiling, add the asparagus and blanch for 1 minute. Lift out and put into a bowl of cold water until the asparagus is cold, then drain. Lay 4 stalks on each mushroom.

Crumble the Boursin on top, then bake the mushrooms for 20 minutes until the cheese has melted.

While the mushrooms are baking, heat the balsamic vinegar in a pot over medium-high and reduce it by half.

Divide the mesclun among 6 serving plates. Set the baked mushrooms on the mesclun. Lightly drizzle the balsamic vinegar over all and serve immediately.

Filo-Crusted Five-Onion Tart with Chèvre

Serves 6 to 8

6	sheets filo pastry	6
½ cup	melted butter	120 mL
2	red onions, finely sliced	2
6–8	cloves garlic, sliced	6–8
1 Tbsp.	butter	15 mL
1 Tbsp.	brown sugar	15 mL
1 Tbsp.	balsamic or red wine vinegar	15 mL
½ tsp.	dried thyme or oregano	2.5 mL
	salt and freshly ground black pepper to taste	
1	leek, sliced	1
1	Spanish onion, white or yellow, sliced	1
1 Tbsp.	butter	15 mL
1 Tbsp.	minced fresh thyme	15 mL
1	bunch green onions, sliced	1
½ lb.	crumbled chèvre	225 g

Set the pastry on a counter to soften. (Wrap unneeded sheets of filo well and store them in their original box in the fridge. They will keep for a week.) Melt the butter. Preheat the oven to 375°F (190°C).

Combine the red onions, garlic, butter, brown sugar, vinegar, thyme or oregano, salt and pepper, and simmer 15 to 30 minutes until the onions are tender. Add water in small amounts as needed to keep the onions from sticking or burning.

In a separate pan over medium-high, sauté the leek and Spanish onion slices in the butter until tender.

Lay a sheet of filo on the counter and brush it with a little of the melted butter. Cover with a second sheet at an offset angle and butter it, then add 4 more sheets, buttering each, to form a large, vaguely pinwheel circle.

Transfer the circle to a baking sheet lined with parchment paper, then layer the red onion mixture, leek-onion mixture, thyme, green onions and chèvre on the centre. Fold the edges into the centre to contain the filling, brush the pastry with more butter, and bake until golden, about 40 minutes. Serve hot.

This is a variant on a staple "new Canadian" favourite I had on the menu at my restaurant, Foodsmith. In the restaurant, I made a quiche-like tart in brisée pastry with a custard of eggs and cream. Here, it is a freeform galette **sans** *eggs and cream. [If you want to make it with the custard, mix together 6 eggs and 2 cups (500 mL) half-and-half cream. Pour the mixture over the onion-cheese layer, which has been spooned into a brisée crust. Bake at 325°F (160°C) until the custard is just set, about 40 minutes.]*

— dee

Chocolate Espresso Milkshake

*A summer favourite among
Caffè Beano customers, this is
as decadent a milkshake
as you will find!*

— Rhondda

Serves 1

1	single shot of espresso, hot	1
⅓ cup	Callebaut chocolate shavings	80 mL
⅓ cup	cold milk	80 mL
3	large scoops vanilla ice cream	3

Melt the chocolate shavings into the espresso. Add the milk to this mixture and combine with the ice cream in a blender.

Cougar's Milk

*The ultimate backcountry skiing
beverage, Cougar's Milk fulfills all
the prerequisites: it's sweet, hot,
lightweight, and has enough
alcohol to warm even the coldest
toes. Believed to have been first
enjoyed by Erling Strom at
Mount Assiniboine Lodge.*

— Rhondda

Serves 1

¼ cup	sweetened condensed milk	60 mL
½ cup	boiling water	120 mL
2 oz.	dark rum	60 mL
	nutmeg to taste	

In a mug, combine the sweetened condensed milk, hot water and rum. Sprinkle with nutmeg and enjoy!

the bakery

Crackers with Coarse Salt & Seeds

Makes about 5 to 6 dozen

1 Tbsp.	yeast	15 mL
2 Tbsp.	brown sugar	30 mL
¼ cup	hot water	60 mL
1 cup	hot milk	240 mL
3 Tbsp.	melted butter	45 mL
1 tsp.	sesame oil	5 mL
1 cup	whole wheat flour	240 mL
1 ½ cups	all-purpose flour	360 mL
⅓ cup	sesame seeds	80 mL
1 Tbsp.	kosher salt	15 mL

Topping No. 1:

1 Tbsp.	butter, melted	15 mL
1 tsp.	coarse salt (kosher or pickling)	5 mL
1 Tbsp.	fennel seeds	15 mL

Topping No. 2:

1 Tbsp.	butter, melted	15 mL
2 Tbsp.	sesame seeds	30 mL
1 tsp.	coarse salt	5 mL

Combine the yeast, brown sugar and hot water in a large bowl or the large workbowl of a countertop mixer. Let stand 5 minutes or so until the yeast activates and bubbles up.

Add the hot milk, melted butter, sesame oil, both flours, sesame seeds and salt. Mix well by hand or with a dough hook, then turn onto the counter to knead by hand. You may need to work in up to ½ cup (120 mL) more all-purpose flour as you knead the dough. Knead with a folding and turning motion for 5 minutes, or until the dough is satiny smooth.

Lightly oil or butter the workbowl, place the dough in the bowl, cover snugly with plastic wrap, and let rise in a warm place until the dough doubles in bulk, about 1 hour.

Preheat the oven to 375ºF (190ºC). Line 3 baking sheets with parchment paper. Punch down the dough and divide it in thirds, leaving ⅔ lightly covered in the mixing bowl.

Flour the counter and roll out $^1/_3$ of the dough with a rolling pin, working towards an even rectangle, as thinly rolled as possible, about 22 x 17 inches (55 x 43 cm). Trim the edges with a large knife or pizza cutter.

Brush the dough with $^2/_3$ of the melted butter from Topping No. 1, then sprinkle with $^2/_3$ of the salt and fennel seeds. Using a large flipper or palette knife, transfer the rectangle to a baking sheet.

Bake for 12 to 20 minutes until crisp and crunchy, depending on how thin the crackers are. Check and turn the pans after 10 minutes. Let the crackers cool on the tray or on a wire rack before breaking them and transferring to a tin or jar, moving them carefully so the seeds don't fall off.

Roll out the remaining dough into two rectangular sheets as for the first sheet. Use the last $^1/_3$ of Topping No. 1 on half a sheet. For the remaining sheet and a half of dough, brush the dough with the melted butter from Topping No. 2, then sprinkle with the sesame seeds and coarse salt. Bake as above.

Savoury Biscotti

Makes 16

1 cup	unsalted butter	240 mL
½ cup	granulated sugar	120 mL
4	eggs	4
3 cups	all-purpose flour	720 mL
1 cup	cornmeal	240 mL
2 tsp.	baking powder	10 mL
1 tsp.	cayenne	5 mL
1 tsp.	black pepper	5 mL
1 Tbsp.	fresh rosemary leaves, chopped	15 mL
4 cups	grated Italian cheese (Fontina, mozzarella, Asiago, provolone)	1 L
1 cup	sunflower seeds	240 mL

Cream together the butter and sugar in a large bowl. Add the eggs and mix well.

In a separate bowl, combine the flour, cornmeal, baking powder, cayenne, pepper, rosemary, cheese and sunflower seeds. Add the dry ingredients to the butter mixture, mixing just enough to combine.

On an oiled or parchment-lined baking sheet, shape into a 5- x 16-inch (12- x 40-cm) rectangle, about 1 inch (2.5 cm) thick.

Preheat the oven to 275ºF (135ºC).

Bake for 40 minutes until firm and golden. Remove from oven and allow to cool.

Using a serrated knife and a sawing motion, cut across the rectangle at 1-inch (2.5-cm) intervals to form 16 biscotti. Bake for 10 minutes.

Yeasted Flatbread or Naan

Makes 10 ovals

1 ½ Tbsp.	yeast	22 mL
2 Tbsp.	white sugar	30 mL
¼ cup	warm water	60 mL
4–4 ½ cups	all-purpose flour	1–1.12 L
1 Tbsp.	kosher salt	15 mL
1 cup	plain yogurt	240 mL
1 cup	buttermilk	240 mL

Combine the yeast, sugar and water in a large bowl or in the bowl of a countertop mixer. Let stand for 5 minutes, or until the yeast foams and bubbles. Add 4 cups (1 L) of the flour, the salt, yogurt and buttermilk. Mix with a sturdy wooden spoon or dough hook, adding the remaining flour as needed. Turn the dough onto the counter and knead well, about 5 minutes, or until the dough is smooth and supple.

Lightly oil the bowl, return the dough to the bowl, cover snugly with plastic wrap, and let stand in a warm place until the dough doubles in size, about 1 hour.

Line the bottom rack of your oven or the rack of your outdoor barbecue with unglazed ceramic tiles. Preheat the tiles for 1 hour at 450°F (230°C), or on high if you are using the barbecue. If you don't have tiles, just place the naan on an inverted baking tray for baking.

Punch down the dough and divide it into 10 equal pieces. Roll each piece out with a rolling pin (or use the heel of your hand for a rougher, more rustic look) into a smooth oval about 4 ½ x 8 inches (11.25 x 20 cm). Transfer each oval to a baking sheet that has been lined with parchment paper or lightly oiled. Let the breads rise 25 to 30 minutes, until doubled in bulk.

Working quickly, transfer the bread ovals to the preheated tiles, using a long-handled flipper. You should be able to fit 4 to 6 naans inside a normal-sized barbecue or oven. Close the door or lid quickly. Check the bread in 3 minutes, lifting from the tile to check the colour on the underside. Flip each oval when golden brown and crusty, then bake another 3 minutes.

Remove the bread to a cooling rack while you cook the remainder. If not serving immediately, cool and wrap well, then freeze until needed. To reheat, wrap each naan in aluminum foil and reheat for 5 to 7 minutes in a hot oven. If you are baking the naan just before you plan to serve it, wrap the baked ovals in kitchen cloths to keep warm.

Oval flatbread conjures up visions of tandoori ovens, the Taj Mahal and spicy foods eaten out of hand. These tender breads are perfect for dips and spreads, too, with a slight tang imparted by yogurt and buttermilk. Set the breads out whole and let your guests tear off pieces, or slice the ovals into tidy rectangles or squares before you set the bread on the table. Like most breads, these naan freeze well, so you can make them in advance.

— dee

Cornmeal Honey Bread

Makes 2 loaves

¾ cup	warm water (105° to 115°F/about 35°C)	180 mL
1 ½ cups	warm buttermilk	360 mL
2 Tbsp.	unsalted butter	30 mL
⅓ cup	honey	80 mL
1 cup	cornmeal	240 mL
¼ cup	toasted sunflower seeds	60 mL
¼ cup	toasted pumpkin seeds	60 mL
1 Tbsp.	instant yeast	15 mL
1 Tbsp.	salt	15 mL
4 ½–5 cups flour		1–1.25 L

In a small pot, heat the water, buttermilk, butter and honey over medium heat until the honey is liquified.

In a large bowl, combine the cornmeal, seeds, yeast, salt and 1 cup (240 mL) flour. With a wooden spoon, mix in the liquid. Gradually add the remaining flour, using only enough to create a soft, unsticky dough. Knead for 3 minutes.

Place in an oiled bowl, cover and allow to rise until doubled in size, about 1 ¼ hours. Punch down and shape into 2 round loaves. Set them on an oiled or parchment-lined baking sheet and let rise for 40 minutes.

Preheat the oven to 350°F (175°C). Bake for 40 minutes, or until golden brown.

gravlax on buckwheat blini with flying fish roe & crème fraîche (page 24)

truffle gnocchi with fried sage & toasted walnuts (page 126)

caramel sticky buns with pecans (page 198)

strawberry frangipane tart with lavender honey crème fraîche (page 220)

Welsh Cakes

Makes about 4 ½ dozen

3 cups	unsifted all-purpose flour	720 mL
1 ½ tsp.	baking powder	7.5 mL
½ tsp.	baking soda	2.5 mL
1 tsp.	salt	5 mL
1 cup	sugar	240 mL
1 tsp.	ground nutmeg	5 mL
¼ tsp.	ground mace	1.2 mL
1 cup	butter	240 mL
¾ cup	currants	180 mL
2	eggs, beaten with 6 Tbsp. (90 mL) milk	2

Sift the dry ingredients together in a large bowl and cut in the butter finely, using 2 knives or a pastry blender. Stir in the currants, then the eggs mixed with milk, to make a stiff dough.

Roll to ¼ inch (.6 cm) thickness on a floured surface. (It's easier to roll out half of the dough at a time.) Cut out rounds with a sharp, round cookie cutter 2 inches (5 cm) in diameter.

Bake on a heated griddle set on low heat, or in an oloctric frying pan set at 350°F (175°C), for 8 to 10 minutes. When golden brown on one side, turn and cook the second side until golden.

Serve cold or hot with butter as a tea cake. Welsh cakes keep remarkably well stored in a covered container.

Also known as Bakestone cakes, these addictive tea cakes were baked by my great-grandmother in her fireplace, either on a griddle hanging from a hob or on a hot, flat stone. My grandmother, Frances Evans, uses an electric frying pan with amazing results! Shortening is satisfactory in this recipe but butter gives a richer flavour and colour.

— Rhondda

Cranberry Apricot Pound Cake

This great standby dessert can be dressed up with fruit compote or good vanilla ice cream and cranberry sauce. The cake may be frozen up to 2 months.

— Rosemary

Makes 2 small loaves

¼ cup	cognac	60 mL
¾ cup	dried apricots, chopped	180 mL
½ cup	dried cranberries	120 mL
3 cups	flour	720 mL
½ tsp.	baking powder	2.5 mL
½ tsp.	baking soda	2.5 mL
½ tsp.	salt	2.5 mL
8 oz.	unsalted butter	225 g
2 cups	sugar	480 mL
2 tsp.	vanilla	10 mL
4	eggs	4
¾ cup	buttermilk	180 mL

Heat the cognac and pour over the apricots and cranberries in a large bowl. Let cool.

Sift together the flour, baking powder, baking soda and salt, and set aside.

In the bowl of an electric mixer, cream the butter. Gradually add the sugar and vanilla and beat until light. Add the eggs one at a time and beat in.

Stir the buttermilk into the fruit mixture. With the mixer on low, alternate adding the dry and wet ingredients to the fruit. Mix just until incorporated, scraping the bottom of the bowl.

Preheat the oven to 325°F (160°C). Spread into 2 greased loaf pans. Bake 50 to 60 minutes. The loaves will shrink away from the sides of the pan.

Vanilla Extract

When buying vanilla extract, be sure the label says "pure vanilla extract," and avoid imitation vanilla flavouring. The alcohol content must be at least 35%, and it should contain no sugar, caramel colour or preservatives.

Extracts are used in dishes whose appearance would be marred by the tiny black seeds of the vanilla bean.

— Gail Norton

Lemon Loaf

Makes 4 loaves

1 ¼ cups	coarsely grated lemon rind	300 mL
⅓ cup	white sugar	80 mL
2 cups	water	480 mL
7 cups	all-purpose flour	1.7 L
3 cups	white sugar	720 mL
¼ cup	baking powder	60 mL
1 Tbsp.	salt	15 mL
½ cup	whole eggs	120 mL
2 cups	milk	480 mL
1 ⅓ cups	half-and-half cream	320 mL
1 cup	lemon juice	240 mL

Bring the lemon rind, ⅓ cup (80 mL) sugar and water to a boil. Simmer for 10 minutes until it forms a syrup. Remove from the heat and set aside to cool.

Mix the flour, 3 cups (720 mL) sugar, baking powder and salt in a separate bowl, then add the lemon rind syrup and blend thoroughly.

In another bowl, combine the eggs, milk, cream and lemon juice. Add to the flour mixture and blend thoroughly. Let stand for 15 to 20 minutes.

Preheat the oven to 325°F (165°C) and grease 4 loaf pans. Scrape the batter into the pans and bake for about 1 hour, until the loaves are golden yellow and the centres spring back when pressed with a finger. Let cool in the pans.

This deliciously moist loaf is a Twin Falls Chalet classic. Many an appreciative hiker has devoured a thick slice of this loaf with a hot cup of tea in the backcountry of Yoho National Park. Make the whole recipe—the extra loaves freeze well for up to 2 months.

— Rhondda

Sour Cream–Blueberry Streusel Coffee Cake

Makes 2 loaves or 9-inch (23-cm) round layers

For the streusel topping:

1 cup	quick oats	240 mL
1 cup	flour	240 mL
1 ⅓ cups	brown sugar	320 mL
¾ cup	melted butter	180 mL

In a large bowl, mix all the topping ingredients just until they start to hold together. Set aside.

For the cake:

1 cup	butter	240 mL
2 cups	sugar	480 mL
2 cups	sour cream	480 mL
5	eggs	5
2 tsp.	vanilla	10 mL
3 cups	flour	720 mL
2 tsp.	baking soda	10 mL
¼ tsp.	salt	1.25 mL
1 cup	fresh or frozen blueberries	240 mL

In a large mixing bowl or in the bowl of a mixer, cream the butter and sugar until smooth. Add the sour cream and eggs and mix well, but do not overwhip or the cake will fall. Add the vanilla.

In a separate bowl, mix together the flour, baking soda and salt. Sprinkle 1 Tbsp. (15 mL) of the flour mixture over the blueberries.

Gradually add the flour mixture to the sour cream mixture until well blended. Gently fold the blueberries into the batter.

Preheat the oven to 350ºF (175ºC). Butter 2 pans or line with parchment paper. Spread the batter into the prepared pans. Sprinkle the streusel over top.

Bake for approximately 50 to 60 minutes until a knife inserted into the centre of the cake comes out clean.

Filo Baskets

Makes 12 baskets

3 sheets	filo pastry	3 sheets
¼ cup	melted unsalted butter	60 mL

Preheat the oven to 375ºF (190ºC). Lay a sheet of pastry on a work surface and brush with butter. Cover with the second sheet, butter it, then repeat with the third. Using a sharp, straight-edged knife, slice the filo into 12 squares. Gently place each square in a muffin pan, ensuring that the corners of the pastry are folded across the top flat surface of the muffin pan to keep the pastry from sliding in.

Bake for about 7 minutes, or until nicely golden brown. Remove from the oven and let cool before removing the pastry from the muffin cups. Store at room temperature.

These lovely little holders take mere minutes to make, minutes that change the tenor and texture of any meal. Fill them with sweets or savouries, but serve them promptly once filled. You can also brush the sheets with maple syrup instead of melted butter, slice them into triangles (or whatever shape you like) and sprinkle with sliced almonds before baking.

— dee

Caramel Sticky Buns with Pecans

These buns have been made in my family for as long as I can remember. My Aunt Alice would make them for holidays and my mom would use the same dough at Christmas to make a coffee cake in the shape of a Christmas tree with candied fruit as decoration. The buns may be made ahead and frozen before baking.

— Rosemary

Makes 18 buns

For the dough:

⅓ cup	water	80 mL
1 ⅓ Tbsp.	yeast	20 mL
1 tsp.	sugar	5 mL
2 cups	milk	480 mL
⅔ cup	butter	160 mL
¼ cup	sugar	60 mL
1 tsp.	salt	5 mL
2	eggs	2
5 ½–7 cups	flour	1.4–1.7 L

Use hot tap water. Put in a mixing bowl and sprinkle the yeast and sugar over top. Let sit until bubbles form, about 5 minutes. This lets you know the yeast is alive and your buns will rise!

Meanwhile, scald the milk in a pot over medium-high heat. In the bowl of a mixer with the paddle attachment, mix the butter, sugar and salt. Add the hot milk, then the eggs. Add the yeast mixture and gradually add flour until a thick, sticky dough forms. Mix well. Use only enough flour for the dough to start to come away from the side of the bowl.

Take the bowl off the mixer and scrape down the dough. Add a bit more flour until it is soft but no longer sticky. Let the dough sit until it doubles in size, about 1 hour.

For the topping:

¼ cup	water	60 mL
½ cup	butter	120 mL
1 cup	brown sugar	240 mL
1 cup	pecans	240 mL

In a saucepan, bring the water, butter and sugar to a boil. Spread the pecans out in two 8-inch (20-cm) square baking pans. Pour the butter mixture over the pecans.

For the filling:

1/2 cup	sugar	120 mL
1 Tbsp.	cinnamon	15 mL
1/2 cup	melted butter	120 mL
1 cup	raisins	240 mL

Mix together the sugar and cinnamon in a bowl.

When the dough has risen, turn it out on a floured surface and roll into a 9- x 24-inch (23- x 60-cm) rectangle. Spread the melted butter on the dough, then sprinkle the cinnamon sugar and raisins over top.

Roll the dough up jelly-roll fashion, starting from the long edge. Cut into 18 individual buns. Place the buns on top of the pecans in the baking pans. Let sit for 20 minutes.

Preheat the oven to 350ºF (175ºC). Bake for 30 minutes until golden. Let cool for 5 minutes, then turn the pans upside down onto a baking sheet and remove the pans.

Blueberry Orange Buns: Use the same bun dough and procedure, but omit the topping. For the filling, use blueberries instead of raisins and add 1 Tbsp. (15 mL) grated orange zest. After rolling and cutting the buns, place them on a baking sheet lined with parchment paper. Bake 30 minutes at 350ºF (175ºC). When cool, make a glaze of 1 cup (240 mL) icing sugar and the juice of one orange. Drizzle over the buns.

Raisin Squares

Makes one 9- x 13-inch (23- x 33-cm) pan

1 cup	butter	240 mL
1 cup	white sugar	240 mL
2 cups	all-purpose flour	480 mL
2 tsp.	baking powder	10 mL
1	egg	1
1 ½ cups	raisins	360 mL
1 Tbsp.	cornstarch	15 mL
½ cup	white sugar	120 mL
1 cup	boiling water	240 mL
1	lemon, juice and zest	1

In a bowl, mix the butter, sugar, flour, baking powder and egg into a crumbly consistency. Divide the dough in 2 pieces and roll out half to line the pan.

Combine the remaining ingredients in a saucepan and boil for 2 minutes. Spread over the dough.

Roll out the remaining crumb mixture, and cover the filling.

Bake at 325ºF (165ºC) for 30 minutes. Let cool before cutting.

Butter Tarts

Makes 2 to 3 dozen

For the filling:

3 Tbsp.	butter	45 mL
2 cups	brown sugar	480 mL
¾ cup	corn syrup (or pure maple syrup)	180 mL
4	eggs	4
1 tsp.	vanilla	5 mL
1 tsp.	lemon juice	5 mL
2 cups	raisins	480 mL

Melt the butter and mix the sugar with it in a large mixing bowl. Add the corn or maple syrup and let cool.

Beat the eggs, vanilla and lemon juice together in a separate bowl, then add to the cooled sugar mixture. Blend well, and add the raisins when the ingredients are nearly combined. Set aside.

For the pastry:

5 ½ cups	unbleached all-purpose flour	1.3 L
1 ½ tsp.	salt	7.5 mL
1 lb.	vegetable shortening	450 g
1	egg	1
1 Tbsp.	white vinegar	15 mL
1 cup	cold water	240 mL

Sift the flour and salt together in a large bowl. Work the shortening into the flour mixture with a pastry cutter.

In a separate bowl, whisk the egg, vinegar and water together. Add the egg mixture to the flour mixture, stirring with a fork until the dough just holds together.

Gather the dough into a ball. On a floured surface, knead the dough briefly, then shape into a ball. Wrap the dough in plastic and refrigerate for at least 1 hour.

Preheat the oven to 325ºF (165ºC). Roll out the pastry and cut into 4-inch (10-cm) rounds. Fit the pastry into muffin pans. Stir the filling well, as the raisins tend to sink to the bottom, then fill each tart nearly to the top with filling.

Bake for about 17 minutes, until lightly golden brown. Let cool in the pans.

Every Canadian family has its own version—some with walnuts and others without raisins. This is my favourite, chewy and sweet. We add a bit of cinnamon and nutmeg when we make them at Caffè Beano.

— Rhondda

Maple Pecan Bars

Makes one 12- x 17-inch (30- x 43-cm) pan

For the crust:

1 ½ cups	butter	360 mL
1 cup	sugar	240 mL
4 cups	flour	960 mL
½ cup	chopped pecans	120 mL

Preheat the oven to 350ºF (175ºC). Mix all the ingredients together in a large mixing bowl or a mixer with the paddle attachment, just until the dough starts to come together. Pat the dough into a 12- x 17-inch (30- x 43-cm) baking sheet lined with parchment paper. Roll with a rolling pin until flat. Bake for 10 minutes.

For the filling:

2 cups	brown sugar	480 mL
½ cup	melted butter	120 mL
6	eggs	6
¾ cup	corn syrup	180 mL
¾ cup	maple syrup	180 mL
¼ tsp.	salt	1.2 mL
2 cups	finely chopped pecans	480 mL
2 cups	coarsely chopped pecans	480 mL

Combine everything except the pecans in a large mixing bowl or a mixer with the paddle attachment. Mix well. Add the nuts and mix again.

Pour the filling onto the prebaked crust. The pan will be very full. Bake for 15 minutes, then rotate the pan. Bake another 10 minutes and check for doneness. The bars are done when the filling is set. Let cool in the pan.

Cream Cheese Brownies

Makes 16 squares

For the cream cheese filling:

8 oz.	cream cheese	225 g
1 ¼ tsp.	flour	6.2 mL
5 Tbsp.	sugar	75 mL
1	egg	1
½ tsp.	vanilla	2.5 mL

Mix all the cream cheese filling ingredients in a food processor just until smooth. Set aside.

For the brownie:

4 oz.	unsweetened chocolate	115 g
8 Tbsp.	unsalted butter	120 mL
1 ¼ cups	sugar	300 mL
½ tsp.	vanilla	2.5 mL
3	eggs	3
¾ cup	flour	180 mL

Gently melt the chocolate and butter together in a double boiler or microwave. Mix the sugar and chocolate mixture in a bowl or a mixer just until combined. Add the vanilla. Then add the eggs 1 at a time, blending each just until mixed. Add the flour and mix by hand until incorporated.

Preheat the oven to 300°F (150°C). Grease an 8-inch (20-cm) square pan.

Spread ⅔ of the brownie mixture into the pan. Spread the cream cheese filling over the brownie. With a spoon, "plop" the remaining brownie mixture evenly over the cream cheese filling. Using the handle of the spoon, swirl the batters together until they're marbled.

Bake 40 to 50 minutes until a knife inserted in the centre comes out clean.

These brownies are for those dessert fans who don't want to choose between cheesecake and brownies—the best of both worlds!

— Rosemary

Beano Biscotti

Makes 5 to 6 dozen

1 ⅛ cups	butter	270 mL
1 cup	white sugar	240 mL
1 ⅓ cups	packed golden yellow sugar	320 mL
2	eggs	2
2 tsp.	vanilla	10 mL
⅓ cup	water	80 mL
4 cups	white flour	950 mL
2 tsp.	cinnamon	10 mL
1 tsp.	salt	5 mL
1 tsp.	baking soda	5 mL
4 ½ cups	oats	1 L
1 ½ cups	raisins	360 mL

In a large bowl, cream the butter and sugars together.
Add the eggs, vanilla and water, and mix until smooth.
Add the flour, cinnamon, salt, baking soda and oats and
mix until well combined. Stir in the raisins last, scooping
the dough from the bottom of the bowl to mix them in
thoroughly.

Preheat the oven to 325ºF (165ºC). For each biscotti,
pinch off a piece of dough and hand-shape a fingerlike
cookie at least 3 inches (7.5 cm) long. Place the biscotti
on an oiled or parchment-lined baking sheet.

Bake for about 17 minutes. The raisins should have
begun to caramelize and the biscotti should be light
brown and crisp right through.

Citrus Shortbread

Makes 2 to 3 dozen

1 Tbsp.	lime zest	15 mL
1 Tbsp.	lemon zest	15 mL
1 Tbsp.	orange zest	15 mL
1 Tbsp.	orange liqueur or juice	15 mL
¾ lb.	unsalted butter	340 g
1 cup	sugar	240 mL
1 cup	flour plus 2 Tbsp.	270 mL
½ tsp.	salt	2.5 mL

In a small bowl, combine the citrus zest with the liqueur.

In a large mixing bowl or the bowl of a mixer with the paddle attachment, beat the butter and sugar until light and not grainy. Add the zest and liqueur.

Gradually add the flour and salt just until well combined. Scrape the bowl a couple of times while mixing to make sure everything is incorporated.

Turn the dough onto a floured surface. Divide into 4 pieces. Roll each piece into logs about 2 inches (5 cm) in diameter. Roll in plastic wrap. Refrigerate for at least 1 hour. (They may also be frozen at this point. Defrost in the refrigerator overnight before baking.)

Preheat the oven to 350°F (175°C). Remove from the refrigerator and unwrap. Slice into ¹/₂-inch (1.2-cm) slices and place on oiled or parchment-lined baking sheets. Bake for 12 to 15 minutes or until just golden around the edges. Let cool on the baking sheets before removing.

For special occasions, we drizzle these cookies with melted white chocolate and decorate with candied violets. They may be stored in an airtight container for 1 week or frozen for 1 month.

One of my favourite cookies! The citrus aroma will fill your kitchen while they bake, and they taste just as good as they smell. I love to make big batches of dough to keep in the freezer and pull out at a moment's notice, or for the holidays.

— Rosemary

Julsterner (Christmas Stars)

Makes about 20 cookies

½ cup	unsalted butter	120 mL
⅓ cup	white sugar	80 mL
½ tsp.	vanilla	2.5 mL
1	egg yolk	1
1 cup	all-purpose flour	240 mL
½ tsp.	baking powder	2.5 mL
	pinch salt	
1	egg white	1
⅓ cup	pecans, toasted and chopped (see page 171)	80 mL
2 Tbsp.	white sugar	30 mL

Preheat the oven to 375ºF (190ºC). Line several baking sheets with parchment.

In a large bowl, cream the butter, then add the sugar and vanilla and cream until light and fluffy, 1 to 2 minutes. Add the egg yolk.

In a separate bowl, sift together the flour, baking powder and salt, and blend into the egg-butter mixture, stirring well.

Whisk the egg white until foamy and set aside.

Stir together the chopped pecans and sugar. Set aside.

Dust the counter with flour and roll out the dough to a thickness of ¼ inch (.6 cm). Cut the dough into 2-inch (5-cm) squares. Place each square on a baking sheet and brush with egg white.

Slice each corner diagonally almost to the centre. Sprinkle the centre with a bit of the sugar-nut mixture. Fold every other point into the centre, forming a star. Bake until golden brown, about 7 to 10 minutes. Cool before moving from the tray.

Baci di Cioccolati

Makes 4 dozen

10 oz.	semisweet chocolate	285 g
⅔ cup	butter	160 mL
3	eggs	3
1 cup	sugar	240 mL
2 tsp.	vanilla	10 mL
¾ cup	flour	180 mL
½ tsp.	baking powder	2.5 mL
	pinch salt	
1 cup	dried cranberries	240 mL
1 cup	dried apricots, chopped	240 mL
1 cup	white chocolate chips	240 mL

Gently melt the chocolate and butter together in a double boiler or microwave. Let cool.

Beat the eggs and sugar together until thick. Add the vanilla and melted chocolate and butter. Stir in the flour, baking powder and salt and mix well. Fold in the dried fruits, then the white chocolate chips.

Preheat the oven to 325ºF (160ºC). Drop by spoonfuls onto a greased or lined cookie sheet. Bake 12 minutes, until the tops are crackly, puffy and shiny. They will remain soft after baking.

Baci in Italian means kiss. This cookie is definitely a kiss of chocolate, with a bonus of white chocolate, cranberries and apricots. A nice holiday treat.

— Rosemary

Peanut Butter, White Chocolate & Pecan Cookies

I've been a P. B. cookie fan since I was a little girl, when my mother let me mark the cookie tops with a fork. This version is even yummier than Mom's. If you want to try another taste treat, try substituting semisweet chocolate and macadamia nuts for the white chocolate and pecans.

— Rosemary

Makes about 3 dozen

1 cup	butter	240 mL
1 cup	brown sugar	240 mL
¾ cup	white sugar	180 mL
2	eggs	2
1 tsp.	vanilla	5 mL
1 ½ Tbsp.	water	22 mL
1 cup	peanut butter	240 mL
2 cups	flour	480 mL
1 tsp.	baking soda	5 mL
½ tsp.	salt	2.5 mL
1 ½ cups	white chocolate chips	360 mL
1 ½ cups	chopped pecans	360 mL

Beat the butter and sugars together. Add the eggs, vanilla and water and mix well. Blend in the peanut butter. Mix in the flour, baking soda and salt, just until combined. Add the chocolate chips and pecans.

Preheat the oven to 350ºF (175ºC). Scoop by spoonfuls onto greased or lined cookie sheets. Press down slightly before baking. Bake 12 minutes, until light golden brown.

desserts & sweets

Macerated Winter Fruits

Good in crêpes, on frozen yogurt or ice cream, on or in baked goods, and in tarts and galettes. Admittedly, ice wine gilds the lily. By all means substitute brandy, Scotch, bourbon, vin santo, or your tipple of preference. For non-alcoholic rehydrators, use good fruit juice. You can substitute different dried fruits, although bigger varieties like apricots and pears need to be slivered to minimize their soft texture on being rehydrated.

— dee

Makes about 1 ½ cups (360 mL)

⅓ cup	dried cranberries	80 mL
⅓ cup	dried sour cherries	80 mL
½ cup	ice wine or late-harvest wine	120 mL

Combine the fruits and wine, stirring often, and let stand, covered, for 4 to 12 hours or until the fruits soften. Add more wine if needed.

Crème Fraîche

Crème fraîche is a thickened, slightly tangy, rich-textured cream used in cooking and for garnishing. In France, unpasteurized cream is used which contains the necessary elements to self-thicken when left at room temperature.

Crème fraîche can be sweetened with sugar or honey, or made savoury with powders or ground spices such as wasabi or cumin. The additions are endless—just remember to add a little of whatever flavouring you are going to use to start and add more in small increments until you get the desired taste. A tiny pinch of salt, whether for sweet or savoury, will help define the flavour.

— Shelley

Makes about 1 cup (240 mL)

1 cup	whipping cream (don't even think of using anything less than 32%)	240 mL
2 Tbsp.	buttermilk or sour cream	30 mL

Place the whipping cream and buttermilk or sour cream in a clean, sterilized glass or stainless-steel container, preferably one that's tall and narrow. Cover and keep in a warm (70°F/140°C) spot for at least 12 hours, and up to 48 hours. You'll see that the mixture becomes very thick.

Stir well, then flavour as desired and refrigerate. Crème fraîche will easily keep for 10 days in the fridge.

Vanilla Crème Fraîche: Whisk a few vanilla seeds or vanilla extract to taste into the thickened crème fraîche.

Praline Brittle

Makes about 1 cup (240 mL)

1 cup	toasted, peeled hazelnuts (see page 171)	240 mL
1 cup	white sugar	240 mL
	water as needed	

Line a baking sheet with aluminum foil, then lightly butter the foil. Spread the nuts over the foil.

In a heavy-bottomed non-reactive pot, combine the sugar with just enough water to help it dissolve. Stir well, then cook over high heat, without stirring, to a dark brown caramel. Swirl the caramel carefully in the pot if it colours unevenly.

When it is dark brown, pour the caramel over the nuts in a thin layer and let cool. Once cooled, break into pieces for brittle.

Praline Powder: Grind pieces of brittle to a fine powder in a food processor. Store in an airtight container in the freezer.

From simple ingredients, greatness arises. Praline is one of the great bartering tools of the kitchen. Use the brittle in small or large pieces in cookies and baked goods. Use praline powder on and in baked desserts, and as a plate garnish.

When ground, it looks like powdered gold, and you should treat it the same way. The nuts can be varied, or blended, to suit your taste, but be sure to toast (and skin, if necessary!) any nuts to get the most flavour for your crunch. This recipe can easily be doubled or tripled, so make much, grind it and freeze it.

— dee

Chocolate Sandwich

One of my hiking specialties, this is a version of a pain au chocolat that will never get crushed in your pack! Bernard Callebaut chocolate bars are to die for but if you're unfortunate enough not to have one of his shops in your area, Zero bars or any Swiss chocolate will do nicely.

— Rhondda

Serves 2

1	fresh baguette (a softer variety is preferable)	1
2 or 3	high-quality chocolate bars	2 or 3

Cut the baguette lengthwise and fill with chocolate pieces. The warmer the day, the tastier the treat. Best enjoyed at the peak.

Truffles

Lumpy and rough-hewn they may be, but truffles—either of the chocolate or the fungus type— are a delicacy and a luxury of the highest order. Of course, the chocolate variety requires neither a truffle-scenting dog or pig, nor a trip to the truffle-yielding oak groves of Perigord or Umbria. What chocolate truffles do require is willpower. Eat one, and you will want more. Hold me back!

— dee

Makes 4 to 5 dozen small truffles

double recipe   Ganache (see page 230)   double recipe

Prepare the ganache and let cool to scooping consistency. Scoop out teaspoonfuls, roll into tidy balls, then roll the balls in Dutch-processed cocoa powder. (I use Pernigotti.) Freeze to store longer than 10 days.

For truffles with crunch, roll the ganache around a toasted and peeled hazelnut, then dredge in cocoa.

Ganache

If this is sitting in your fridge, you have "instant anything" chocolate. Melt and stir into coffee or hot milk. Use it as a sauce on crêpes. Use it as a filling or a glaze. Take it to bed with your darling and some beautiful berries. Use it to buy favours and pay debts. Bribe children (or maybe not!).

It keeps, refrigerated, for about two weeks. Reheat gently in the microwave on low power or over simmering water to bring to usable consistency.

— dee Hobsbawn-Smith

Malted Milk Chocolate Ice Cream

Serves 4 to 6

3 cups	homogenized milk	720 mL
6 oz.	Callebaut milk chocolate, chopped	170 g
2 oz.	Callebaut dark chocolate, chopped	56 g
1 cup	whipping cream	240 mL
1 cup	liquid barley malt	240 mL
4	egg yolks	4

Melt both chocolates with 1 cup (240 mL) milk gently in a microwave (medium heat for no longer than 3-minute intervals, stirring in between). Alternatively, chop the chocolate in small pieces and melt over a double boiler, with the water just at a simmer.

Heat the remaining milk with the whipping cream in a pot over medium-high to scald.

Combine the malt and yolks in a large mixing bowl. When the cream is steaming, slowly whisk it into the yolk mixture, stirring constantly. Pour it back into the pot. Heat over medium-high, stirring constantly with a wooden spoon until the mixture coats the back of a spoon.

Strain into the chocolate mixture and stir to combine. Chill and process in an ice cream maker according to the manufacturer's directions.

I've been trying to create a malt-flavoured ice cream ever since I had one at Tribeca Grill in New York City years ago. For all those people who grew up eating Malted Milk Balls or the malts from the Bay, here you go!

— Pam

Caramel Crème Fraîche Ice Cream

Serves 4 to 6

1 cup	granulated sugar	240 mL
1 cup	whipping cream	240 mL
1 cup	homogenized milk	240 mL
8	egg yolks	8
1 recipe	Crème Fraîche	1 recipe

Melt the sugar in a heavy-bottomed pot over high heat until the sugar is liquid and deeply caramelized but not burnt, about 5 to 10 minutes. Carefully pour the cream into the pot, stirring as it bubbles up. Add the milk and lower the heat to medium-high. Cook until it is smooth again, stirring constantly.

Place the yolks in a mixing bowl. Slowly whisk the caramel mixture into the yolks, stirring constantly. Return to the pot and cook over medium-high heat, stirring constantly with a wooden spoon until the mixture is slightly thickened and coats the back of a spoon, about 5 to 10 minutes. Immediately strain into a clean bowl. Stir in the crème fraîche and chill several hours or overnight.

Process in an ice cream maker according to the manufacturer's directions.

Crème Fraîche

Makes 2 cups (480 mL)

¾ cup	sour cream	180 mL
1 ¼ cups	whipping cream	300 mL

In a non-reactive bowl, whisk the creams together to smooth out any lumps. Cover loosely and leave at room temperature overnight. The next day, cover and refrigerate to store.

Backcountry Sherry Trifle

Serves 8

1	stale cake or jelly roll	1
3–4 Tbsp.	sherry	45–60 mL
1	package flavoured Jello	1
1	14-oz. (398-mL) can fruit salad	1
2 1/2 cups	prepared custard	600 mL
1 cup	whipping cream	240 mL

Cut the cake into small squares and line the bottom of a deep bowl with the pieces. Slosh the sherry over top until the cake is moistened.

Make the Jello, using 1/2 water and 1/2 fruit juice from the canned fruit. Pour over the cake and set in the refrigerator until firm, about 1 to 2 hours.

When the Jello is firm, spoon the fruit salad over top, then pour the custard on top of the fruit. Return to the refrigerator for another hour or two, until it is firmly set.

Whip the cream and spoon dollops of cream on top of the trifle before serving.

A quick and easy trifle that's perfect when you're away from town and need a dessert made from non-perishables—or when you just don't feel like going to the store! I use Bird's custard powder for a simple backcountry treat. Feel free to substitute fresh fruit such as raspberries, which are traditional, or bananas. If you don't want to use Jello, you can replace it with 1/2 cup (120 mL) of your favourite jam.

— Rhondda

Apple & Pear Ginger Crêpes

Serves 4 to 6

For the ginger crêpes:

⅔ cup	flour	160 mL
¼ cup	sugar	60 mL
2 tsp.	ground ginger	10 mL
¼ tsp.	salt	1.25 mL
1 cup	milk plus 2 Tbsp.	270 mL
4	eggs	4
5 Tbsp.	Ginger Butter	75 mL

Combine the dry ingredients. In a separate bowl, whisk together the milk, eggs and ginger butter. Whisk in the dry ingredients until relatively smooth. Let the batter rest for at least 30 minutes, whisk again and strain before using.

When ready, heat an 8-inch (20-cm) non-stick pan (or two, if you can manage) on medium-high and begin making crêpes. Using a small ladle, pour batter into a well-oiled pan. I keep a dish with some oil and a brush handy to brush the pan as needed. Swirl the batter to distribute evenly over the bottom of the pan. After 1 to 2 minutes, flip over and cook the crêpe until it is only slightly coloured on both sides.

Begin a stack, separating each crêpe with a square of waxed or parchment paper. You will probably have to adjust the heat as you go along. Once you've found your stride, this will not seem so daunting a task and eventually using two pans will be a snap.

Your crêpes can be tucked inside a resealable plastic bag (still separated) and frozen for future use. Just thaw them in the refrigerator overnight.

For the caramelized apples and pears:

4 Tbsp.	unsalted butter	60 mL
3	medium dense apples, peeled, cored and cut into 8 or 10 slices each	3
3	medium Bosc or hard winter pears, peeled, cored and cut into 8 or 10 slices each	3
¾ cup	sugar	180 mL
¼ cup	whipping cream	60 mL

Heat the butter in a large, heavy skillet on medium-high until it sizzles. Add the apples and pears and cover with the sugar. Don't stir; instead, leave to caramelize for 5 or 10 minutes. Only then, toss gently, and continue to sauté another 5 minutes until the fruit is tender. Add the cream and stir gently. Cool slightly.

To serve, put a heaping spoonful of caramelized fruit on one side of each crêpe and fold the crêpe into quarters. Serve with a good vanilla or cinnamon ice cream, crystallized ginger and mint sprigs.

Ginger Butter

Makes about 1 cup (240 mL)

8 oz.	unsalted butter	225 g
3 oz.	grated fresh ginger	85 g

Bring the butter and ginger to a boil in a small saucepan. Remove from the heat, skim and strain through a fine sieve.

Strawberry Frangipane Tart with
Lavender Honey Crème Fraîche

*Follow the seasons with this
tart: strawberries, pitted
cherries, apricots, peaches,
plums, raspberries, apples,
pears . . . The pastry is based
on a recipe by Carol Field. It
makes enough dough for two
10-inch (25-cm) tarts. You can
freeze half of the dough for
a future dessert.*

— Pam

Serves 8 to 12

For the sweet pastry:

2 ¼ cups	flour	535 mL
½ cup	sugar	120 mL
½ tsp.	salt	2.5 mL
1 ¾ cups	unsalted butter, slightly softened	425 mL
1	large egg	1
1 tsp.	pure vanilla	5 mL

By hand:

Combine the flour, sugar and salt in a large bowl. Cut in the butter with a pastry blender or 2 knives until you have a coarse, meal-like texture. Combine the egg and vanilla in a separate bowl. Mix into the flour-butter mixture, squeezing with your hands until the dough holds together. Shape into 2 disks, wrap separately and chill for at least 1 hour.

With a mixer:

Cream the butter and sugar together using the paddle attachment of the mixer. Add the egg and vanilla and mix well. Combine the flour and salt and mix into the dough just until the dough comes together. Shape into 2 disks, wrap separately and chill for at least 1 hour.

For the frangipane:

³/₄ cup	ground almonds	180 mL
¹/₂ cup	granulated sugar	120 mL
1 tsp.	bitter almond extract	5 mL
1	large egg	1
¹/₄ cup	unsalted butter, softened	60 mL
¹/₄ cup	flour	60 mL
2 cups	strawberries, washed and hulled	480 mL
¹/₂ cup	sliced almonds	120 mL

In a mixer or large bowl, combine the ground almonds and sugar. Add the almond extract and egg, blending until smooth. Add the softened butter, a bit at a time, and blend with a spoon or paddle to a paste. Scrape down the mixing bowl. Add the flour and mix just until incorporated.

Preheat the oven to 350°F (175°C). Roll out 1 disk of pastry dough and fit into an 11-inch (27-cm) tart pan with a removable bottom. Prick the bottom and bake for 10 minutes.

Spread the frangipane mixture evenly in the baked tart shell. Cut the strawberries in half and arrange attractively over the frangipane. Sprinkle sliced almonds around the edge and bake for approximately 45 minutes, until the filling springs back in the centre of the tart. It should have a cakelike consistency.

Let cool and serve slightly warm or at room temperature, with a dollop of Lavender Honey Crème Fraîche on the side. Refrigerate any leftovers, but bring it to room temperature to serve.

Lavender Honey Crème Fraîche

This makes more than enough lavender honey for the tart. The remaining honey is delicious spread on toast, as a sweetener for whipped cream, in homemade ice cream, drizzled over fresh figs...

Makes about 2 cups (480 mL)

1 cup	honey	240 mL
1 Tbsp.	lavender blossoms, unsprayed	15 mL
½ recipe	Crème Fraîche (see page 216)	½ recipe

Place the honey in a pot. Add the lavender blossoms. Bring to a boil, stirring once to distribute the lavender. Remove from the heat and allow to cool in the pot for a couple of hours. Reheat slightly to reliquify the honey and strain into a jar.

In a bowl, combine the crème fraîche with 5 Tbsp. (75 mL) of the lavender honey. Combine and refrigerate, covered, until ready to serve.

Coconut Raspberry Tartlets

Makes six 4-inch (10-cm) tarts

For the tart pastry:

13 Tbsp.	unsalted butter	195 mL
⅓ cup	icing sugar	80 mL
1	large egg yolk	1
1 ½ cups	flour	360 mL
1 Tbsp.	half-and-half or whipping cream	15 mL

You can use a mixer, a food processor, or your hands to make this dough. The key is to work quickly and not overdo the mixing. You want the dough just to come together. Then wrap it in plastic and chill for 30 minutes. You will need six 4-inch (10-cm) tart shells with removable bottoms.

When slightly chilled, set the dough on a floured surface. Cut into 6 pieces. Roll the dough into 5-inch (13-cm) circles. Fit the rolled dough into the pans, folding the dough down onto itself inside the pans. Chill for 20 minutes.

Preheat the oven to 350ºF (175ºC). Place the tart shells on a baking sheet and bake for 10 minutes or until light golden. If the bottoms puff up during baking, press them down so you will have a flat bottom for filling. Let cool.

For the filling:

¾ cup	sugar	180 mL
1 cup	half-and-half or whipping cream	240 mL
2 cups	fresh raspberries	480 mL
1 ½ cups	unsweetened shredded coconut	360 mL

Combine the sugar and cream in a saucepan over medium heat and stir until the sugar dissolves, about 5 minutes. Let cool 10 minutes.

Combine the berries and coconut in a bowl. Gently stir in the cream mixture. The filling should not be runny and the coconut should just be moistened. Spoon the filling into the prebaked tart shells, mounding it toward the centre.

Bake 20 to 25 minutes, until the coconut is just beginning to toast. Let cool completely before removing from the pans.

Almond Ricotta Torte

Serves 8 to 12

8	large eggs, separated	8
½ cup	sultana raisins, soaked in a bit of brandy or grappa	120 mL
2 cups	sugar	480 mL
2 cups	fresh ricotta cheese	480 mL
2 cups	finely ground skinless almonds	480 mL
1 tsp.	lemon zest	5 mL

Preheat the oven to 375°F (190°C). Butter and flour a 10-inch (25-cm) springform pan and set aside. Beat the egg whites until stiff and set aside.

Drain the raisins (making sure you drink the brandy or grappa as the chef's treat!). Combine the egg yolks, raisins, sugar, ricotta, almonds and lemon zest. Gently fold the egg whites into the almond mixture.

Pour into the springform pan and bake in the lower third of the oven for about 1 hour. Allow to cool for 15 minutes in the pan before releasing it onto a pretty plate. Cool completely and serve with a little cream and fruit, depending on the season.

Many years ago, a neighbour shared the original version of this incredible cheesecake with me and I have been making it ever since.

— Ellen

Grinding Nuts
To finely grind nuts, add several spoonfuls of the allotted amount of sugar to the nuts while grinding them in your food processor.

— dee Hobsbawn-Smith

Lemon-Lime Raspberry Cheesecake

Serves 8

For the crust:

1 ¼ cups flour		300 mL
⅓ cup	icing sugar	80 mL
½ cup	butter	120 mL

Using your hands or a food processor, mix the ingredients just until they come together. Press into a 10-inch (25-cm) greased springform pan, starting at the bottom and working halfway up the sides. Bake at 350°F (175°C) for 12 minutes.

For the filling:

1 ½ lbs.	cream cheese	680 g
1 cup	sugar	240 mL
1 cup	sour cream	240 mL
1 tsp.	vanilla	5 mL
4	eggs	4
1 tsp.	lemon zest	5 mL
1 tsp.	lime zest	5 mL
1 recipe	Citrus Curd	1 recipe
1 cup	raspberries	240 mL

Bring the cream cheese to room temperature. Beat the sugar and cream cheese together by hand or in a mixer with a whisk attachment until smooth but not fluffy. Beat in the sour cream and vanilla. Add the eggs one at a time. Add the zest and ¹/₂ cup (120 mL) Citrus Curd.

Sprinkle the raspberries into the prebaked crust. Pour the cream cheese batter over the berries. Swirl ¹/₂ cup (120 mL) Citrus Curd over top.

Preheat the oven to 325°F (160°C). Bake for 40 minutes. The cake should be set, but still wobbly. If not, bake 10 minutes more. Turn off the oven and leave the cheesecake in the oven for 20 minutes. Refrigerate at least 5 hours before removing from the pan.

Serve with a spoonful of the remaining curd.

Citrus Curd

Makes about 2 ⅔ cups (640 mL)

⅔ cup	butter	160 mL
¾ cup	sugar	180 mL
4	eggs	4
¾ cup	mixed lemon and lime juice	180 mL
	zest of 2 lemons and 2 limes	

If necessary, add bottled lemon or lime juice to make up ³/₄ cup (180 mL) of juice.

Melt the butter. In a food processor, process the sugar and eggs. Add the melted butter. Add the juice and zest. Put into a glass measuring cup. Microwave, stirring every minute until thick, about 5 minutes. Chill.

Hazelnut Torte with Ginger-Lime Cream

The torte in this dessert is rolled up to encase the filling like an old-fashioned jelly roll, with spectacular and contemporary results. The entire thing can be frozen and served semi-thawed, alla semifreddo, or it can be chilled and served when set. Entirely different desserts result by using ground pistachios paired with raspberry purée folded into whipped cream; almonds with chocolate ganache; almonds with lemon curd; or hazelnuts paired with coffee or chocolate whipped cream. The torte can also be baked in a springform pan instead of on a flat baking sheet, then split and layered with any of the suggested fillings.

— dee

Makes 2 tortes, each serving 12 to 16

4 cups	finely ground hazelnuts	1 L
1 ¼ tsp.	baking powder	6.2 mL
12	eggs, separated	12
1 ⅓ cups	white sugar	320 mL
2 Tbsp.	brandy	30 mL
1 recipe	Ginger-Lime Cream	1 recipe

Line two 12- x 15-inch (30- x 37.5-cm) baking sheets with parchment paper. Preheat the oven to 350°F (175°C).

Combine the nuts and baking powder. Set aside.

Whip the egg whites on high speed until stiff peaks are formed. Gently transfer the whipped whites to a large non-reactive bowl. Whisk the yolks and sugar with the brandy until the yolks are tripled in volume and pale in colour.

Fold ¼ of the yolk mixture into the egg whites. Add ⅓ of the remaining yolks and ⅓ of the nut mixture and fold in. Repeat with the remaining yolks and nuts over two additions.

Divide the mixture evenly over the two trays, smoothing gently with a whisk. Bake about 15 minutes, or until just set.

Unfold two clean kitchen cloths (each larger than the pans) onto the counter. Dust generously with icing sugar. As soon as the pans are removed from the oven, invert a pan onto each cloth and remove the pan. Using a small sharp knife to peel the edges free, remove the parchment. Roll the torte in the towel and place on a rack to cool completely. Repeat with the second torte.

To assemble, gently unroll the tortes and cover with the Ginger-Lime Cream. Roll up and gently transfer to a platter. Dust with icing sugar if desired. Chill thoroughly. Slice when very cold, with a hot wet knife that is cleaned between each slice.

Ginger-Lime Cream

Makes about 4 cups (1 L)

5	eggs	5
1 cup	white sugar	240 mL
¼ cup	unsalted butter, melted	60 mL
1 cup	fresh lime juice	240 mL
	zest of 2 limes	
4 Tbsp.	grated ginger root	60 mL
2 cups	whipping cream	480 mL
1 Tbsp.	icing sugar	15 mL

Whisk together the eggs and sugar in a non-reactive bowl. Add the butter, lime juice, zest and ginger. Mix well.

Transfer to a pot and continue whisking. Cook over medium-high heat, whisking constantly. When thick but not boiling, strain through a sieve into a clean bowl. Cover closely with plastic, putting the plastic directly onto the surface of the curd to prevent a skin forming. Poke a few holes in the plastic to allow steam to escape. Let cool, then chill.

Whip the cream and icing sugar to firm peaks. Fold into the cold curd.

Scotch-Apricot Chocolate Pecan Torte

This recipe evolved from a cover recipe on **Bon Appetit** many years ago. If you want to make a showstopper dessert, add the chocolate glaze and curls. But this torte is also pretty wonderful by itself or simply dusted with icing sugar or cocoa powder.

— Rosemary

Serves 12

½ cup	scotch whisky	120 mL
1 ¼ cups	dried apricots, chopped	300 mL
1 cup	sugar	240 mL
¾ cup	butter	180 mL
5	eggs	5
½ Tbsp.	vanilla	7.5 mL
8 oz.	semisweet chocolate	225 g
⅓ cup	graham cracker crumbs	80 mL
1 ½ cups	pecans, toasted and chopped (see page 171)	360 mL
¼ cup	flour	60 mL
1 recipe	Chocolate Glaze	1 recipe
	4- x 6- x 1-inch (10- x 15- x 3-cm) slab semisweet or bittersweet chocolate (for curls to garnish)	

Preheat the oven to 350ºF (175ºC). Grease and flour a 10-inch (25-cm) springform pan. Heat the scotch and pour over the apricots. Let cool.

Melt the 8 oz. (225 g) chocolate gently over a double boiler or in a microwave.

In a large mixing bowl or the bowl of a mixer with the paddle attachment, beat the sugar and butter until creamy. Add the eggs and vanilla. Add the melted chocolate. Don't worry if the batter looks curdled. Mix in the crumbs, pecans and flour. Gently stir in the apricots and scotch.

Spread into the prepared pan. Bake for 30 minutes. The cake will rise and crack around the edges, and will be soft in the middle. Remove from the oven and let cool completely in the pan. It will sink as it cools.

Set the cake on a serving plate, carefully removing the bottom and sides.

At this point, you can freeze the torte, well wrapped, for up to 1 month. Thaw it in the refrigerator, still wrapped, for at least 6 hours before serving.

Spread with Chocolate Glaze before topping with curls.

To make the chocolate curls, place the chocolate on a plate and microwave for 15 seconds. Turn the chocolate over and microwave 15 seconds more. When the surface just begins to feel soft, take a vegetable peeler and pull across the surface to make curls.

Garnish the torte with the curls. Refrigerate the cake if it will be more than 2 hours before serving time.

Chocolate Glaze

This glaze is also irresistible spread warm over ice cream or brownies.

Makes about 2 cups (480 mL)

1 cup	whipping cream	240 mL
8 oz.	semisweet chocolate, chopped small	225 g

Heat the cream almost to boiling. Remove from the heat. Pour over the chocolate in a bowl. Whisk until the chocolate is melted and totally incorporated. Let cool until the glaze starts to thicken. Pour the warm glaze over the torte. If you want a smooth top, take a spreading spatula and, with a steady quick movement, pull the spatula across the top of the torte while the glaze is still warm.

dee's Flourless Chocolate Cake with Espresso Anglaise

Some kitchens call this a fallen soufflé cake; others call it a mousse cake or a molten lava cake. Regardless of the title, the trick is underbaking, so that it can be served hot with a liquid core or chilled, with a dense and fudgy core. Use the best chocolate you can find for the cake— I am partial to Callebaut and Valrhona. For a simple and dramatic approach, serve with a fruit coulis, ganache or anglaise on the side.

Personally, I like the cake best chilled, dusted with icing sugar and cocoa, garnished with chocolate ganache and raspberry coulis.

— dee

Serves 12

1 lb.	semisweet chocolate, shaved	450 g
½ cup	unsalted butter	120 g
8	large eggs, separated	8
1 cup	white sugar	240 mL
¼ cup	espresso or very strong coffee	60 mL
1 recipe	Espresso Anglaise	1 recipe
1 recipe	Raspberry Coulis with Chambord	1 recipe
1 recipe	Chocolate Mousse	1 recipe
1 recipe	Ganache	1 recipe

Preheat the oven to 325ºF (160ºC). Butter and flour a 10-inch (25-cm) springform pan. Make an aluminum foil collar and fit it around the pan.

Melt the chocolate and butter on medium power in the microwave, stirring every 2 minutes, or over hot (not boiling) water on the stove, stirring constantly.

Beat the egg whites in a clean bowl until stiff but not dry. Set aside.

Beat the yolks on high speed, adding the sugar and espresso, until tripled in volume and pale in colour.

Fold the melted chocolate and butter into the egg yolks, stopping before it is completely incorporated. Fold in the egg whites over three additions.

Gently pour the batter into the pan and bake 40 to 50 minutes. The cake should look just underdone. Let cool a few minutes, then loosen the cake's sides from the pan with a small knife. When the cake is cool, remove the springform sides.

To serve, place a slice of cake on each plate. Drizzle the ganache over the cake, spoon the anglaise and the coulis around the cake and, using two spoons, scoop an egg-shaped mound of mousse onto the plate.

Ganache

Makes about 1 cup (250 mL)

4 oz.	semi-sweet chocolate	120 g
½ cup	whipping cream	120 mL
2 Tbsp.	espresso or coffee liqueur	30 mL

Melt the chocolate over hot water or on low power in the microwave. Heat the cream to just above body temperature. Stir the cream and espresso or liqueur gently into the chocolate, adding all at once. You can use this as a glaze or a sauce.

Espresso Anglaise

You can vary the flavour of the anglaise by replacing the coffee with mint sprigs, grated nutmeg, maple syrup, thyme and lemon zest, cinnamon sticks, allspice berries, good vanilla (added at the end of the cooking period), or good cognac.

Makes about 2 ¹/₂ cups (625 mL)

4	egg yolks	4
¹/₃ cup	white sugar	80 mL
¹/₄ cup	espresso	60 mL
2 cups	half-and-half cream	480 mL

Whisk together the yolks and sugar until light and fluffy. In a heavy-bottomed pot over medium-high, heat the espresso and cream until hot but not boiling. Add ¹/₄ of the hot coffee-cream blend to the yolk-sugar mixture, whisking well. Stir in the remaining coffee and cream. Transfer the mixture back to the pot and cook over medium-high heat until thickened but not boiling. Strain, cover and chill. Serve cold.

Raspberry Coulis with Chambord

Makes about 2 cups (480 mL)

2 cups	raspberries, fresh or frozen (unsweetened)	480 mL
2 Tbsp.	sugar, or to taste	30 mL
1–2 Tbsp.	Chambord, or to taste	15–30 mL
1–2 Tbsp.	lemon juice, or to taste	15–30 mL

Thaw the berries if frozen. Sieve them, discarding the seeds. Stir in the remaining ingredients. Chill.

Chocolate Mousse

Makes about 4 cups (1 L)

¾ lb.	semisweet chocolate, chopped	340 g
½ cup	boiling milk	120 mL
2 Tbsp.	white sugar	30 mL
3 Tbsp.	safflower, sunflower or other neutral-flavoured oil	45 mL
1 ½ cups	whipping cream	360 mL
2 Tbsp.	dark or amber rum	30 mL
2 Tbsp.	vanilla or espresso	30 mL

Combine the chocolate, milk, sugar and oil in a food processor equipped with a steel knife. Blend thoroughly. Whip the cream to firm peaks and fold in the remaining ingredients by hand. Chill.

Three-Chocolate Mousse Torte with Raspberry Coulis

Very rich, but not too sweet—and stunning to look at. This may look complicated, but it's not. Your guests will be amazed. This dessert is lovely by itself, but I think raspberries put it in a class above. When in season, I just sprinkle fresh raspberries on top of the plates when I serve.

— Rosemary

Serves 12 to 16

For the chocolate base:

4 oz.	semisweet chocolate, melted	115 g

Line a 10-inch (25-cm) springform pan with plastic wrap. Pour the chocolate into the pan, and spread over the bottom only. This chocolate gives a base for the mousse to sit upon. It doesn't need to be perfectly smooth; it just needs to cover the bottom of the pan. Chill for 10 minutes.

When hard, remove the chocolate disk from the pan. Turn over and put the chocolate disk back into the pan, then peel the plastic wrap off.

For the dark chocolate mousse:

10 oz.	semisweet chocolate	285 g
4 oz.	unsalted butter	115 g
4	eggs, separated	4
1 tsp.	instant coffee dissolved in 2 tsp. (10 mL) water	5 mL
⅛ tsp.	cream of tartar	.6 mL
2 Tbsp.	sugar	30 mL

Gently melt the chocolate and butter together in a double boiler or microwave. When melted and smooth, whisk in the egg yolks and coffee.

Beat the egg whites with the cream of tartar until soft peaks form. While beating, slowly pour in the sugar, and beat until stiff but not dry.

Whisk ⅓ of the egg whites into the chocolate mixture. Fold the remaining whites gently into the mixture. Scrape the mousse into the springform pan. Wipe the side of the pan above the mousse, so the next layers will be clean. Refrigerate or set in the freezer while the next layer is prepared.

For the coffee–milk chocolate mousse:

9 oz.	milk chocolate, chopped	250 g
3 tsp.	instant coffee dissolved in ¼ cup (60 mL) water	15 mL
1 ½ cups whipping cream		360 mL

Carefully melt the chocolate and coffee together in a double boiler or microwave. Milk chocolate burns very easily, so stir it often and remove from the heat as soon as it starts to melt.

Whip the cream just past the soft peak stage. It should be firm but not stiff. Fold gently into the chocolate.

Spread on top of the dark chocolate mousse. You should have about ³⁄₄ inch (2 cm) left for the top layer. If not, remove a bit of the milk chocolate mousse—this can be your treat. Wipe the side of the pan above the mousse and refrigerate or set in the freezer while you prepare the next layer.

For the white chocolate mousse:

¼ cup	water	60 mL
9 oz.	white chocolate, chopped	250 g
1 ½ cups	whipping cream	360 mL

Melt the chocolate with the water in a double boiler. White chocolate is fragile, so stir often and remove from the heat as soon as it starts to melt.

Whip the cream until firm but not stiff. Gently fold the cream and chocolate together. This mousse will be soft.

Pour the white chocolate mousse on top of the milk chocolate mousse, and level the top of the mousse with a metal spatula or spreader. Refrigerate overnight or for at least 6 hours before serving.

Remove the torte from the pan by heating a metal spatula under hot water and running it around the inside of the springform pan. Remove the ring. Gently slide the torte onto a serving platter. Use a hot knife to cut and serve individual pieces. Spoon Raspberry Coulis onto each serving plate, then set a slice of mousse tarte on top.

Raspberry Coulis

Makes about 3 cups (720 mL)

20 oz.	frozen raspberries, thawed	600 g
½ cup	sugar	120 mL

Purée the berries and sugar in a food processor. Strain to remove seeds. Refrigerate for up to 3 days.

Dessert for Jackson Pollock

Each component of this dish can be made days in advance, then combined just before service for a richly spectacular dessert. It had its beginnings as I was planning my share of our annual New Year's Eve dinner; it was finally my year to do dessert, but it had to be portable. I made each piece ahead of time, packed it all up and put it together inside of five minutes at our friends' home with a suitable fanfare of New Year's trumpets. The mousse makes more than this dish needs, so use the extra for plain mousse, frozen for a semifreddo, as a filling for a layer cake—or for a private chocolate party with your nearest and dearest!

— dee

Serves 12 generously

½ cup	whipping cream	120 mL
½ cup	white sugar	120 mL
8	large egg yolks	8
2 cups	whipping cream	500 mL
½ lb.	bittersweet Callebaut chocolate, chopped	225 g
6 Tbsp.	Frangelico or other hazelnut liqueur	90 mL
½ cup	finely chopped toasted hazelnuts (see page 171)	120 mL
12	Filo Baskets (see page 197)	12
¾ cup	Ganache, melted (see page 230)	180 mL
12	Truffles (see page 214)	12
12 pieces	Praline Brittle (see page 213)	12 pieces
¾ cup	Macerated Winter Fruits (see page 212)	180 mL
¾ cup	Praline Powder (see page 213)	180 mL

To make the mousse, heat the ¹/₂ cup (120 mL) cream to just below boiling point. Keep warm.

Heat the sugar in a second pot over medium-high, with just enough water to dissolve the sugar (about ¼ cup/60 mL), mixing well, then allow to caramelize to dark brown. Remove from the heat and carefully add the heated cream. It will boil up vigorously, so use caution.

Add a small amount of the caramel to the egg yolks, mix well, then return the egg mixture to the rest of the caramel. Using a candy thermometer to regulate the temperature, cook the caramel-yolk mixture to 160°F (70°C), stirring constantly.

Strain the mixture through a fine-mesh sieve, then whisk it in a mixer until the caramel is cool.

Whip the cream to firm peaks. Melt the chocolate on low power in the microwave or in a double boiler, stirring frequently.

Add the liqueur to the cooled caramel, then fold in the melted chocolate. Fold in the whipped cream, then the chopped hazelnuts.

When ready to serve, centre a filo basket on each plate. Melt the ganache on medium power in the microwave or over hot water on the stove. Spoon 1 Tbsp. (15 mL) melted ganache into the bottom of each basket, reserving a small amount for garnish.

Using a piping bag, pipe 2 to 4 Tbsp. (30 to 60 mL) of mousse on top of the ganache in a circular pattern. Top the mousse with a truffle and a triangle of hazelnut brittle. Scatter 1 Tbsp. (15 mL) macerated fruits about each filo cup. Using a long-tined fork, rapidly flick melted ganache over each plate for a splatter-paint look, then dust with praline powder. Serve immediately.

index

index